The Hopeful Mom's Guide to Adoption

The Hopeful Mom's Guide to Adoption

THE WIT & WISDOM YOU NEED FOR THE JOURNEY

Rachel Garlinghouse

ISBN-13: 9781546929918
ISBN-10: 1546929916
Library of Congress Control Number: 2017908757
CreateSpace Independent Publishing Platform
North Charleston, South Carolina

Acknowledgements

There are so many who helped make this book go from a dream to a reality. Roll call!

To **my husband** who took over caring for our four children, as soon as he got home from work, so I could write, edit, and check Facebook. (Hey, everyone needs a break, right?) He's steadfast, encouraging, and supportive. And most of all, he said yes, four times, when I told him, "I want to adopt a baby." There is no one else I want to do life with.

To **my four children**, the loves of my life. I am thrilled to be your mom, your kitchen dance party DJ, your sneaker of chocolate chips, and your cheerleader. I love you as big as the sky.

To **my childrens' birth families**. I'm honored that you chose me and my husband to be your child's forever family. I hope we've made you proud.

To **my dad** who told me to write every day and **my mom** who instilled in me a love of reading.

To **my little sister** who always posts encouraging (and inappropriately funny) things on social media in support of my endeavors. And to **my little brother** for always laughing at my "that's what she said" jokes.

To **my adoption and foster care triad support group**. I would be lost without you.

To **Madeleine Melcher**, my friend and co-author of *Encouragement for the Adoption and Parenting Journey*, for kicking me in the proverbial rear so I'd get this book written. And for all the wisdom she pours into my life.

To my graphic designer, **Natalie Smith**. She helped me create two beautiful books. She's smart and kind.

To **my in-laws and cousins and aunts and uncles and friends** who've cheered me on through every writing and adoption journey. And **to Grandma** who passed away while I was completing this book. I hope reading this would have made her proud.

To **my friend Casey** for watching my babies for me so I could run home and furiously write this manuscript.

To **the women who have poured their hearts into making me a better mommy** to my Black daughters: Bria, Jazmine, Emma, Rachel, and Gwen. They've encouraged, advised, and loved big.

To **Jennifer, Jackie, and Shelley,** the women who will talk adoption and motherhood with me any time of day or night (literally), and who love my family as their own.

To **Haagen-Dazs**, for making java chip ice cream. To **Starbucks** for sugar-free lattes. To **St. Louis Bread Co**. for iced coffee. To caffeine in general. And champagne. Cheese fries. You've all helped make this book possible. Cheers!

A Not-So-Fluffy Letter to My Readers

Dear Reader,

Thank you for picking up a copy of *The Hopeful Mom's Guide to Adoption*. Grab yourself some cake (not just a piece, honey, but the whole pan), put on your favorite ugly-cozy pants and twenty-year-old tee, and plop down on the couch. We're about to have some fun.

First, you must know, this isn't your typical guide to adopting. This isn't a textbook with bolded vocabulary words, graphs, and research, all typed in six-point font on thousands of pages.

This also isn't a memoir in which I pour out my heart and every little detail of my adoption journey, leaving you sobbing. Why? Because you don't care. You are trying to forge your own path. Sure, I give you enough information to connect with me, but I'm not going to talk to you about my favorite brand of tampons. We aren't *that* connected. And as for the sobbing, I'm sure if you are thinking about adopting, you've done your fair share of sobbing. (Spoiler alert: you're going to do a whole lot more before you have a baby in your arms.)

This also isn't a "how to" book. There are plenty of those. They have shady titles like *How to Get a Baby Faster Than You Can Sneeze* and include tips like "use James

1:27 in your plea for money from relatives and friends in order to fund your adoption." The cover usually features a couple who look like they are on a travel-to-the-Bahamas brochure: tanned, perfectly straight and glaringly bright white teeth, and toned arms draped over one another. Standing between them is the most gorgeous child you've ever seen, a child who looks like she never forgets her manners, drops French fries into the crevices of the minivan, or poops. They are perfect-perfect-perfect, and your family can be too, if you just buy the book!

In all seriousness, there are adoption books that exist that are incredibly helpful and lovely. I list many throughout this book. I even wrote two of them: *Come Rain or Come Shine: A White Parent's Guide to Adopting and Parenting Black Children* (2013) and *Encouragement for the Adoption and Parenting Journey: 52 Devotions and a Journal* (co-authored with Madeleine Melcher, published in 2015). Unlike my other two adoption-themed books, this one is a bit, er, different.

I recall reading only one funny-helpful book during my first adoption journey, and it was incredibly memorable. That book was *Secret Thoughts of an Adoptive Mother*, written by Jana Wolff. To this day, I have women waiting to adopt share with me how much they adored Jana's transparency and humor. Her book is a jewel, a rare glimpse of the irony, humor, and heartache that comes with choosing to adopt in a world that continues to rank DNA and pregnancy above adoption. This book is in the spirit of Jana's: it's a tropical cocktail among a selection of artificially flavored waters.

Don't we all just want the good stuff? Straight up? Right now? We crave truth, comradery, and a good laugh. Adoption is so serious. Sometimes stiff. Bittersweet and complex. The journey is rocky and unpredictable. We *need* relief. We need someone to say, "Girl! Calm down! Here, have some chocolate. Want to watch a movie with me where Ryan Gosling takes his shirt off?"

I'm here to hand you some chocolate. (Unfortunately, Ryan Gosling hasn't responded to my tweets.)

Are you ready?

In laughter, love, and sweetness,
Rachel

About the Author

E very great book includes an author bio. It's required. It's where the author writes, in the third person (as if an outside person wrote the bio), all of his or her accomplishments so that the reader will be super impressed and will hopefully purchase no fewer than eighteen copies of the book to zealously distribute to their nearest and dearest.

I'm not going to pretend someone else is writing this for me. It's just me. I don't have an assistant or a boss or even any really well-known friends who will make you gasp in admiration.[1] And if my kids were asked to write this, they'd probably talk about my obsession with cooking scrambled eggs for all meals, my ample backside in which they have coined "not fancy," and how mean I am because I refuse to let them drink soda and have televisions in their bedrooms.

Here's what I want you to know about me:

- I have a type A personality. That means I'm punctual, prepared, and organized. I'm often anxiety ridden. I'm a control freak. I RSVP

---

1 I have met Nicholas Sparks (um, can you say "Noah can renovate my house any day"?), caught a glimpse of Luke Perry (yes, the *Beverly Hills 92010* guy; the show I wasn't ever allowed to watch because my mom said it was inappropriate) on a movie set when I was in grade school, and spotted Peter Krause walking down the sidewalk in NYC a few years ago. However, I couldn't remember his name and spent an hour researching online until I stumbled upon his photo on a smutty celebrity gossip website. Now that you are thoroughly impressed, please continue.

the day I get an invitation, buy Christmas gifts in August, and utilize a coupon binder. I am working on this, unsuccessfully.

- I'm a mom of four via adoption. All our adoptions are domestic, open, and transracial. Do you know what adopting does to a person? It makes you amp up your control issues by 1,000,000,000. Meanwhile, adoption's epic-evil-echo laugh mocks you because you have 0% control over it. Adoption is God's opportunity to offer you some humble pie. Grab your fork, Sister. Unless you are diabetic.[2] Then you can just look at the pie yearningly while everyone else eats it.

- I believe in empathy and afternoon tea (though I'm not British). When I expect a guest, I sweep my floors, clean the bathroom, light a candle, and make some dark chocolate brownies. I make my children formally introduce themselves to new friends, including a hand shake and a "nice to meet you." I still handwrite thank you notes and send them via snail mail with stickers on the envelopes. I despise the f-word: fart. Of course, my children chant it no fewer than sixty times a day while laughing hysterically. I really like old movies[3] where the ladies wear pearls and lipstick, despite the fact that I own only a single tube of lipstick (that's very likely to be considered expired) and there are no strands of pearls in my jewelry box.

- I cannot stand when strangers ask me if my kids are "real" siblings, if their birth parents were on drugs, or why I didn't have my "own" children. Look up Mama Bear in the dictionary, and you'll see my name. I have walked away, mid-conversation, from nosy people. I have body-blocked middle-age white ladies trying to touch my daughters' intricate cornrows. And I have told busy-bodies that my children's adoption stories are none of their business. I like to booty-dance like nobody's business, in my

2 Ok, now before you get your panties in a wad over me saying something about diabetics, you should know I am one. Type 1 for eleven years and counting.
3 If you haven't yet, watch Every Girl Should Be Married. It's adorable! And then watch the sequel, Room for One More, because it's adoption themed.

kitchen, in my yoga pants. I think *The Office*, *Bridesmaids*, and the Shopaholic and Bridget Jones books are incredibly funny. I love Jesus, as the t-shirt says, but I do cuss a *little*. And I think worse.

- I absolutely love writing about adoption. My adoption experiences and education have been featured on NPR, MSNBC, CNN, CBS, Huffington Post Live, Scary Mommy, abcnews.com, Yahoo! News, Babble, Medium, Adoptimist, America Adopts, Canada Adopts, Huffington Post, Portrait of Adoption, Fatherly, The Good Men Project, The Mighty, My Brown Baby, Essence magazine, and many, many more.
- I've written five books (before this one) and counting. Two are children's books: *Black Girls Can: An Empowering Story of Yesterdays and Todays* and *Poems for the Smart, Spunky, and Sensational Black Girl*. Two are for adults and talk about adoption: *Come Rain or Come Shine: A White Parent's Guide to Adopting and Parenting Black Children* and *Encouragement for the Adoption and Parenting Journey: 52 Devotions and a Journal* (co-authored with Madeleine Melcher). And then a book on education: *Homeschooling Your Young Black Child: A Getting-Started Guide and Workbook*. I have written all of these during the early morning hours while everyone else slept.
- Before I became a mostly stay-at-home-mom and writer, I taught composition part-time at university for eight years. (Don't judge my social media posts based on my former life in academia. I'm now a mom of four, I have Mommy Brain, the end.) I adored my students, the classroom energy, and the on-campus Starbucks. I have a piece of paper that says I have a master's degree in Teaching of Writing, but what I love about teaching is that it's more about learning.

If you'd like to learn more about my family's adoption adventures, please stop my blog, *White Sugar, Brown Sugar* and say hello. There you'll find all my social media links and much more.

Now that I've proven I'm legit, I'm going to wow you with chapters and chapters of information that will lift your spirits, make you ask hard questions, and prompt you to get a Twitter account if you haven't already, because celebrity Twitter battles are a great distraction. Let's get at it, friend!

In the Beginning

H ere you are. Holding this book. You might be feeling scared, nervous, confused, skeptical, elated, uncertain, relieved, paralyzed, cautiously optimistic, or a combination of some of these. One thing you aren't feeling is carefree.

And really, who can blame you? Choosing adoption, or even thinking about choosing adoption, is overwhelming. It's like you have a cup and a pitcher of water. Well, since we're being honest, it's more like a glass and a bottle of wine. As you pour the liquid, the glass fills quickly and the excess spills over the rim, splashing onto the counter, and dribbling onto the floor. It quickly begins to stain the rug. And then you notice some managed to also stain your brand-new shirt. It's a *bit* of a mess. What started out as simply wanting a glass of wine resulted in disarray.

Welcome to adoption. It's messy. It's complicated. It's frustrating. It goes places you weren't prepared for, no matter how calculated, how educated, and how even-keeled you are.

Adoption: it's a big, beautiful, bittersweet mess.

Vegan Lasagna Will Get You Knocked Up

Let's take a moment to hear from Over-Enthusiastic, Intrusive, Know-It-All, Pet-Fanatic, and Skeptic, shall we?

- "Oh, you're adopting! Just like Sandra Bullock! You know, I read in my *People* magazine last month that...."
- "So you can't have your own kids?"
- "Have you tried burning aromatherapy candles during sex, sticking to an organic-gluten-free-vegan diet, and standing on your head for twenty minutes after having sex while listening to instrumental Chinese music?"
- "Cool! I adopted a cat last year. Best thing I ever did! Feels so good to rescue a little one who needs a good home!"
- "Are you sure adoption is a good idea? My best friend's second cousin's co-worker adopted a kid, and the kid is really jacked up. Has some serious issues."

If you have even hinted that you are considering adoption, chances are you've heard many responses from family, friends, co-workers, and neighbors. Most of these individuals are well-intentioned-but-absolutely-clueless.

Certainly these responses sting a little. Because no matter why you are choosing adoption, it's likely that loss is involved. Loss is the starting point. The game-changer.

People choose adoption for a variety of reasons. Infertility (including secondary infertility) is one of the most common, but it isn't the sole reason. There are people like me who have a condition, disease, or prognosis that can make pregnancy dangerous or impossible. There are those who simply desire to add to their family through the process of adoption because they feel "called" to do so. Some have lost children through miscarriage or infant death. Others have faced the loss of a child they were fostering who returned to his or her biological family.

And let's not leave out the other two parties in the adoption triad: the biological parents and the adoptee (person who was adopted). They have their own losses, too. More on this later.

Adoption doesn't exist without loss. Let's talk more about this after you bake that vegan lasagna.

Broken & Messy

Choosing adoption doesn't eradicate the loss(es) that brought you to this point. Because of this, it's very, very important that you have dealt with the loss(es) you have thus far encountered and experienced before you proceed.

Here's what you need to know:

- A child you adopt isn't a replacement for another child you have lost.
- A child you adopt shouldn't come with special roles to fill as a means of helping you heal.
- A child you adopt has one job: to be a child.
- A child you adopt may experience confusion, anger, and sadness relating to his or her adoption.
- A child you adopt has two families: one by birth and one by adoption.
- A child you adopt is going to look to you for answers.
- A child you adopt is your real child.
- A child you adopt will be a blend of nature and nurture.
- A child you adopt will be an individual who needs to be loved, accepted, supported, and encouraged.

Because of these things, your child is going to need some things from you:

- Empathy
- Honesty
- Openness
- Willingness
- Commitment
- Authenticity
- Confidence
- Vulnerability
- Transparency

In order to meet the needs of your child, you are going to need to enter into adoption having dealt with the past, the broken, messy, heartbreaking past that brought you to adoption.

This doesn't mean that the past will not resurface, that you won't forever mourn the loss of a child who has passed away or who went home, or that you won't sometimes feel things like anger, jealousy, or uncertainty. However, dealing with loss and allowing yourself to work through grief organically and productively will mean you are best prepared to fully embrace the adoption process and the child you adopt.

Each person's grief-journey is different. Because of this, I'm offering a variety of suggestions on the avenues you might embrace to help work through grief:

- Professional counselor
- Infertility, child-loss, and/or adoption support group
- Spiritual leader
- Partner
- Friends
- Family members

Helpful habits:

- Journaling
- Exercising
- Vacationing/stay-cationing
- De-cluttering/organizing/simplifying

- Learning (a new skill)
- Resting/rejuvenating
- Volunteering

Whatever magical combination you discover that works for you, make it a priority and do it! Self-care should always make the top of your to-do list.

I Just Can't Adult Today

As you try to figure out your path, here are some things that aren't helpful:

- Watching any adoption-themed Lifetime or Hallmark movies. The Lifetime movies hardly ever end well and the Hallmark movies will leave you weepy for days. (As if you need to be more weepy!)
- Giving your calendar the middle finger every Mother's Day, setting fire to the Mother's Day cards at your local store, or screaming, "I hate all you fertile bee-ot-ches" at church on Mother's Day. You will not make friends in these ways, and you will very likely wind up in jail.[4]
- Becoming a recluse. Spending every weekend and evening on your couch, eating bags of potato chips, and binge-watching the aforementioned Hallmark and Lifetime movies.
- Insulting all your pregnant or mother friends and family members by refusing to attend any baby showers, child birthday parties, or social events where children or pregger-ladies are present. The women who you are surrounded with now will be the women bringing you gifts when your baby arrives.

---

4 Going to jail is NOT good for your homestudy process. A criminal record doesn't exactly scream qualified-to-adopt-a-human-child. Plus, black and white stripes only make us look wider, ladies. And jail means no more raw cookie dough fests. There are so many reasons to stay out of jail!

- Lying to yourself and others. "How are you?" they ask. "Fine," you reply with a fake smile on your face and ice cream stains all over your t-shirt.
- While sitting in medical office waiting rooms, you find yourself ripping the covers off all the pregnancy and parenting magazines and making paper airplanes out of them, which you proceed to aim and then fly at pregnant women, mothers, and cherub children.
- Privately (or publicly) ranking the cuteness of other people's kids out of jealousy, never giving any kid over a five.
- Take your margarita to the children's clothing department and walk around fingering all the adorable sleepers while sobbing hysterically.
- Act like Miss Hannigan or Cruella DeVill or any of the Real Housewives. It's not cute.

Grief takes time. It doesn't have a deadline. It might be a life-long process. And that is okay.

Hold Your Horses, Girl

There are times in one's life that are more ideal than others to adopt. Here are some instances in which you do not want to move forward with adoption:

- Any major life changes: job, moving, major illness, divorce or separation, caring for a very ill family member.
- When you are having a knee-jerk reaction to bad fertility (or other) news.
- When you aren't financially stable. Adoption, as you are probably aware, can be costly. And parenting a child is expensive.
- When you aren't committed to adoption and the adoption process. You don't have to be 100% sure adoption is right for you (most people who head into the adoption process have some reasonable doubts, insecurities, and confusion), but you cannot be walking two different paths simultaneously and believe it's going to pan out well for all parties involved, especially the child.
- If you are unwilling or unable to make the changes your child may require. This may mean if you are adopting transracially, being willing to move towns, for example, to a more racially diverse area. This may mean making major changes to your work schedule to accommodate the many appointments a child with special needs may have.

- When you and your partner aren't on the same page…like, not even in the same book, like not even in the library together. Adoption is a bumpy ride, and you will need the support of one another and a strong commitment to the journey before your proceed.

I get it. Being told "not now" might make you throw this book at the next moving being that saunters by. (Please don't do this. It's unkind and crazy.) Listen, "not now" isn't "not ever." Don't act like a sulky teenager.

There is No "I" in Team

Are you seriously considering adoption or have you already committed to the adoption journey, but your partner is hesitating? Been there, done that, friend. This chapter is for you.

I knew we would adopt three days after I was diagnosed with an auto-immune disease. One minute, it was just my husband and me listening to a Certified Diabetes Nurse Educator talk to me about calculating carbohydrate grams and injecting insulin. The next minute, when the CDNE asked us if we planned on having children and proceeded to explain what pregnancy with diabetes would involve, I knew we'd adopt. Yes, just like that. I never hesitated, questioned, or had second-thoughts.

But my husband. Let me tell you. He's detail-oriented, practical, and analytical. He's the guy who reads the fine print on every contract, scans credit card receipts before signing on the dotted line, and takes six hours (it feels like) to order food at a restaurant. Decision-making is not his strength.

For a year and a half, we discussed adopting. It was torture for me. I was ready to roll. We'd been married five years, we were established in our careers, we had a house and two cars, and we'd grown out of the honeymoon period. I was ready to settle down, moving past the "first comes love, then comes marriage" part of the song and onto "then comes the baby in the baby carriage." (I never understood the "Steve and Rachel sitting in a tree. K-I-S-S-I-N-G" part. Why would we be sitting in a tree and simultaneously kissing?)

Finally, my husband agreed to attend an adoption informational meeting at a local agency. While he took copious notes and studied the glossy brochures and stapled info packets, I was thinking about my favorite baby names. On the drive home, I told him, "I'm so excited! In less than a year, our baby could be in our arms!" to which he said, "I'm not certain." Thus, he squelched the baby name discussion, and my heart.

This happened time and time and time again in different forms. The night before our first homestudy visit from our social worker in which she'd inspect our home and interview us, my husband said to me, "I'm not sure I want to adopt." (I have never been so angry with him in my entire life. To this day, I'll occasionally bring up this marital moment so we can have a good laugh).

When it came to transracial adoption, special needs adoption, and open adoption, my husband vocalized his fears, doubts, and questions. And I would respond with a resource (a blog post or book chapter), with a get-together (conveniently with a family-by-adoption), or with a guilt-inducing-faith statement about putting it in God's hands (even though, truth be told, I was scared too).

Here's the deal. Struggle isn't bad. Questions aren't wrong. Doubts aren't weaknesses. You need to approach adoption as a team. This doesn't mean you are 100% certain that adoption is right for you or that it'll all be OK. It means you are weak when your partner is strong, and you are strong when your partner is weak. You commit to one another and your future baby.

My husband will readily admit, I was the leader on each of our adoption journeys. I said when it was time to adopt again, I coordinated the get-togethers with birth family, I set up most of the meetings with our social workers. But what did my man do? Oh, did he step up. For example, with our fourth child, we were with her from the minute she was born until we left the hospital with her, by request of her birth parents. My husband spent every night at the hospital, sitting in the NICU (and sometimes standing, for hours, when they were out of chairs) feeding our baby every two hours, surrounded by the beeps of monitors from nearby incubators. My husband knew I needed a lot of rest (thank you, chronic illness).

The thing is, we are all good at different things. Because of my husband's analytical abilities, he helped ensure that the agency and attorney were on the "up and up" (aka: ethics). Because of my dedication and motivation, we were able to complete a homestudy in a timely manner. Because my husband is quieter and more of a "sit back and see" kind of guy, he was able to notice things about the journey and about our kids' families that I didn't. Because of my passion and energy, I was able to start a local adoption triad support group for women (that's grown to over four hundred and twenty five members!).

There's a difference between bumps in the road and a road that's completely awash. Work through struggles, but don't discount your partner's feelings. Sometimes the answer is to wait-and-see versus plow through as quickly as possible. Please believe me when I say this: every delay happens for a reason. Every "no" or "not yet" is a gift. Once your child is in your arms, you will know exactly what I mean.

Now go find a tree, climb up in it with your partner, and have fun K-I-S-S-I-N-G. Hit me up with that photo on Insta. Caption it #WeirdThingsToDoWhileWaitingToAdopt and tag me @whitebrownsugar. Just kidding. Sort of.

Makin' Whoopee

I married my husband at the ripe old age of twenty-one. I remember being asked about our family plans at our reception. (I guess "first comes love and then comes marriage" should be followed up nine months later with "then comes the baby in the baby carriage.") I think we probably disappointed some people when our first baby didn't arrive until we had been married over five years.

When people won't go mind their own damn business and insist on knowing what's going on with your sex life, your fertility, and your "future plans," you can shut them up by saying something (well, really just thinking) like:[5]

- I'm choosing not to have a biological baby for fear he or she will resemble my mother-in-law.
- My husband prefers my derrière to be stretch-mark free.
- I like my perky boobs.
- I greatly enjoy happy hour. Pregnancy interferes with this.
- Have you seen pregnant women? They look like marshmallows.
- Whisper: You mean to tell me that you have to have S-E-X to get pregnant?

---

[5] I assure you that practicing these aloud, preferably with your partner, makes for a great date night activity!

- We cannot figure out this sex-thing. Can you offer me a detailed explanation, please? In a very loud voice? Drawings and puppets would be helpful.
- I've seen how your kids act, and I've decided, wholeheartedly, I do not want or like children.
- Come to find out, you have to have a uterus to carry a baby! Wow. I really screwed that one up!
- Give up sleeping in on weekends, eating sushi, and couples-only vacation resorts? No, thanks!

But if you wish to be dignified, you might say:

- That's personal.
- We'll become parents when we are ready.
- We're having so much fun, just the two of us!
- We're considering adoption as the way to build our family.
- Infertility has been a struggle for us. I appreciate your sensitivity on this matter.
- We plan to have children one day, we just aren't sure when yet.

You will be asked many questions (and offered PLENTY of unsolicited advice) all throughout your parenting journey, so prepare yourself. Perhaps take an improv class to improve your reaction time or arm yourself with throwing stars (like one of my favorite TV characters ever, Dwight Shrute from *The Office*). Who doesn't love the element of surprise? Or, when it doubt, a good old hold-your-breath-until-you-pass-out works for pre-schoolers. Give it a whirl, lady!

Pulling the Trigger

I f you are gun shy, you'll get over it quickly, because your adoption race, ahem, journey, is about to start. Lace up your proverbial running shoes, stretch, and carb-load (that's a thing, right?)[6], and then stand at the starting line.

On your mark? Get set! Go!

Go where? How quickly? Sprint or steady jog? Damn, this is uncomfortable! One minute it's too sunny. The next, it's raining cats and dogs. The pavement is uneven. Out of breath! Blisters! Partner falling behind or getting way too far ahead? Where is the freaking bench?!?

Welcome to adoption, sister!

So now you have to choose an adoption route. Sounds fun, right?

Many people outside the adoption world put adoption into two categories: domestic and international. However, there are many types of adoption including:

- <u>Domestic infant adoption</u>: Using an agency, facilitator/consultant, and/or an attorney, you adopt an infant.

---

6 One thing you should know about me is that I do not run. I do not enjoy it: the boobs flopping about, the sweating, the burning throat and lungs, my hair coming out of a ponytail. So though I may sometimes carb-load, it has everything to do with stress-eating or a low blood sugar and nothing to do with the torturous act of running.

- <u>International adoption</u>: You adopt a child from a country that isn't your own. Commonly, children adopted internationally are over a year old and many have special needs ranging from mild to severe.
- <u>Foster-to-adopt</u> (adoption): Using an agency, you adopt a child who is legally free for adoption from the domestic foster care system. When an infant is placed in a foster home, the goal is reunification with the biological family. If this isn't possible, the next preference is for the child to go into the care of a biological relative. The third possibility is that the child goes into a foster home and possibly becomes available for adoption down the road.
- <u>Embryo adoption</u>: You adopt an embryo conceived by another couple to either "grow" yourself or have placed in a surrogate mother.
- <u>Relative (or familial) adoption</u>: You adopt a relative of yours, such as a niece or nephew, a cousin's child, or a sibling.

Avenues of "adoption" I do not consider anything like adopting a human baby:

- Adopting a pet from a rescue animal shelter.
- Adopting a highway.
- Adopting a family in need for the Christmas season.
- Adopting a penguin at the local zoo.
- Adopting a star and naming it after your partner.

For the sake of this book, I'm focusing on adopting an infant, a child age twelve months or younger, domestically (United States); however, many of the things discussed can apply to adoptions beyond infancy and children adopted from other countries.

Practical Schmatical

Here are some things to consider when choosing which adoption route to take:

- **What will your employer or work schedule allow?** International adoption sometimes requires lengthy out-of-country stays and multiple trips. Adopting within the United States may also require lengthy stays away from home, such as the case if you adopt from another state. You will go through a process called ICPC (inter-state adoption compact) where your home state and the baby's home state have to agree that all the adoption terms have been met and you are approved to bring your baby home.
- **What can you afford?** Adoption can be expensive, and it's not just the homestudy fee and placement fee to consider. There are legal fees, travel expenses, potential birth parent expenses, and post-placement services. Adoptions can cost nothing to nearly-nothing (in the case of foster-care adoption) to over $40,000 (some domestic and international adoptions).
- **How willing are you to support and nurture an adoptee from the particular route you are choosing?** For example, if you live in a 99% white community, yet you wish to adopt a Hispanic child, are you willing to move to a more diverse area for the well-being of your child? If you are pursuing a special needs adoption, what resources do you have in place for you and your child?

- **Where do you live?** How close are you to medical service facilities that your child may need? How are the local schools? Will your child be in a community with children who share his or her race or ability?
- **What are the laws?** Every state has different legal guidelines in terms of TPR (termination of parental rights), ICPC (interstate adoption compact), the birth father's rights, and more.
- **What are the agency's stipulations and do you meet them?** Some agencies have marriage-length requirements, religious requirements, age requirements, etc.
- **What's your heart saying?** Choosing an adoption route because it's cheaper, seemingly easier, etc. doesn't mean it's the right route for you. Which type of adoption makes your heart skip a beat? Where are you being "pulled"?[7] Which adoption route will be most supported by your nearest and dearest?

Only you (and your partner) can answer these questions. So many families go around surveying other families-by-adoption about their experiences with particular agencies or adoption routes, making decisions based on those conversations. Though the experiences of those around you do have value, they aren't adoption gospel. At the end of the day, you have to live with your choices, and more importantly, your choices forever impact and shape the life of a child.

---

7 Please note, I listed this last for a reason. You see, so many people approach me and say things like, "It's SO cool you adopted! I've always wanted to adopt a little Black baby!" Or, "Oh my gosh! Aren't bi-racial kids just the cutest?" Or I've heard, "Down syndrome kids are just so happy and adorable!" (These, by the way, are fetishizing statements and are inappropriate, not to mention quite uncomfortable conversations.) You need to carefully examine your motives, and look at adoption with your head AND your heart.

Peace Be with You

f you haven't been living under a rock, you've probably read or heard the term "ethics" in relation to adoption. What is an ethical adoption? What constitutes as ethical adoption practices?

This is something very important to me. All wine, chocolate, and celebrity Twitter battles aside, we need to have a serious girlfriend chat about ethics. And here's why: *The adoption choices you make today will impact your family, especially your child, forever.*

What you need to acknowledge if you intend to be part of an ethical adoption:

- Adoptive parents are the privileged party in many adoption situations; they are the ones in a financial position to afford adoption. With great privilege comes great responsibility.
- What is right isn't always easy. What is easy isn't always right. It's cliché and true.
- You will almost always know what the right choice is; you just have to have the courage to follow-through.
- All triad members deserve your respect, attention, and empathy.
- You have the right and the responsibility to walk away from any situation (or adoption professional) that is unethical or inappropriate.

- An expectant mother (and father) has every right to parent their child, no matter what their plans and feelings were pre-birth. A match isn't a promise or a guarantee.[8]
- Being overbearing, entitled, demanding, and intrusive with the expectant parents you are matched with is coercion. You do not own the expectant parents or the child they are carrying.
- Today's choices have life-long importance and effects.

You want to be able to convey to your child one day, without a single twinge of guilt and conviction, that you acted ethically every step of the way, that you did nothing coercive or manipulative to sway the birth parents' choice.

I will tell you from personal experience, nothing feels better than knowing my husband and I put ethics above our personal desire to become parents. When we have adoption conversations with our children, we can hold their hands, look in their eyes, and speak with them with our hearts and minds clear of unnecessary heart-hurricanes.

---

8 I know, your control issues are revving up just reading this.

There are No Stupid Questions

I can hear your exasperated sigh. I can see you face planting into that pile of adoption applications on your dining room table. I can hear your car's squealing tires as you dash off to the grocery store to buy a key lime pie so you can eat your feelings.

This is a lot to take in, isn't it?

I promise you, I'm not sharing this to rain on your parade. I don't know you, but I care about the well-being of you, your family, and your future family. Therefore, it would be absolutely careless of me not to share with you the truths I have experienced. So cut a big slice of pie and keep reading, please.

How can you be part of an ethical adoption? I mean, that bullet-pointed list offered in the previous chapter is humbling and thought-provoking, but practically, how does one go about adopting in an ethical way?

First and foremost, choose your adoption professional wisely. Many prospective parents ask valid questions, but they only scratch the surface. Questions that are necessary include:

- What are your fees? What is your fee schedule?
- How many placements do you facilitate a year?
- What are the qualifications a person or couple must have to use your agency?
- How do you support and educate hopeful parents during the homestudy and waiting process?

- How long, on-average, does a person or couple wait with your agency before being matched or placed?
- How do you handle matches?
- Is there a match meeting?
- Are we notified every time our profile is shown?
- What kind of profile do your families create?
- How do you decide which prospective parents are shown to expectant moms?
- How easy are you to get in touch with? What is your communication policy?
- How far along in a mom's pregnancy do you show her waiting family profiles? How far along in a mom's pregnancy do you allow her to match with a family?
- What is the time frame to complete a homestudy?
- How many post-placement visits are required?
- What is your grievance policy?
- May I have a list of three or more references from people who have used your agency in the past?[9]

In addition, you need to ask:

- Who handles the parental rights of the birth mother and birth father? What are the laws and guidelines surrounding TPR, revocation, and finalization?
- How do you counsel expectant parents? What sources of support do you offer them before, during, and after placement?
- How do you support moms who choose to parent, who change their adoption plans?
- How do you support prospective parents who face a long wait, a failed placement, or a difficult match?
- How do you support adoptees?

---

9 Of course, keep in mind the agency isn't going to hand over the names and phone numbers of unsatisfied clients. However, if the agency hesitates or refuses to give you references, that's a red flag.

- Do you help triad members negotiate and maintain openness after the placement? How? For how long after placement?
- What is your policy on paying expectant parent expenses?
- Does the agency offer separate representation for the mom and the intended parents, or is that social worker one in the same?
- Which fees are due at what points in the adoption journey? Which of these are refundable or transferable? Which fees are optional?
- How do you handle situations where a family might wish to change social workers within the agency due to conflicts?

If an agency promises these, run:

- A fairly exact time from waiting to placement.
- A high percentage of moms placing (vs. parenting).
- An easy journey.
- A nonchalant, disinterested, or disengaged approach to your fears or concerns.
- A lack of empathy for birth parents, expectant parents, or adoptees.
- A dismissal of birth parents' rights, including the birth father.
- An intention to get parents to terminate their rights at the exact moment it's legally allowed, versus going situation-by-situation, giving the biological parents the time and respect they need to make the best decision they can for their child.

As you can tell, I encourage you to "ask away." An ethical agency will have no problem taking the time and energy to be forthcoming and transparent.

Random PSAs on Choosing an Adoption Professional

Well, that title was self-explanatory, wasn't it? Let's get at it:

- An agency that uses "Christian" in the title shouldn't be assumed to be operating ethically by default. Make like an archeologist and start digging.
- Paying more money for an adoption doesn't guarantee better service or ethics or a faster placement. Again, do your research.
- If your attorney dresses like Sophia Vergara, as in, dripping with diamonds, wearing four inch cheetah-print heels, and sporting a skin-tight, V-neck to the naval dress, perhaps you need to question their fees.
- Likewise, if your agency, upon first meeting, offers you $5 bottled water and oysters (pearls included) along with a coupon for a complimentary hot stone massage at Hotel You-Can-Never-Even-Afford-to-Rent-the-Cleaning-Closet, question where that $10,000 "get started on finding your cherub child" fee is going.
- Test the waters on availability. If a social worker's response time is unreasonable, consider how those same workers might treat expectant or birth parents and adoptees, especially when requesting post-placement services.
- Scour the agency's website. Are they using appropriate adoption terminology? Do they have a long list of the "pros" of placing but a short list of "cons" of parenting under the "birth parents" tab?

What is your general sense of their agency from the website? Any red flags? Any inconsistencies between what's on the website and what you're told by the social worker you get connected with? Note: Not every agency has a stellar website. If it has basic contact info, some history, and some information, that doesn't mean the agency isn't "good." All three of our agencies had current but unimpressive (AKA: basic) websites.

I know you're ready to roll, thus why you're reading this book. But slow down and "make good choices" (as I tell my kids 1000x a day). You'll be glad you did.

I Hate Red Tape, and I Cannot Lie

E very adoption, and I mean *every* adoption, has some surprises and some setbacks.[10] Red tape is inevitable. The sooner you accept this, the happier you will be. Here are some tips when it comes to keeping your proverbial ducks in a row when the poop hits the fan:

- Keep copies and/or screenshots of all your paperwork, e-mails and texts when it comes to your adoption process. Being organized and having access to information is crucial.
- Make sure you do everything required of you throughout the process and allow ample time for processes to be completed.[11] There can always be delays. If you wait until the last minute to complete a required document or schedule an interview, don't be surprised if issues arise.
- Communicate with your adoption professionals in the ways that work best for them: text, e-mail, by phone, in person. Ask that they do the same for you. And if things aren't going well, you have every right to refer to the agency's grievance policy.

---

10 If you come across someone who says adopting is the easiest thing she's ever done while she tosses glitter and organic candy into the air, you can confidently consider her a liar. I recommend sprinting away from said person. She is not your friend.

11 You aren't Queen Bey. No one is rolling out a red carpet for you, handing you diamonds, and making sure the inside of your limo is a perfect 73 degrees. There are rules, and you need to follow them. The sooner you accept this, the better off you'll be.

- Do not, and I repeat, do not lose your cool. If you are frustrated, a good adoption professional will be right there beside you working to help resolve the issue. Though it's easy to turn on the nearest person, remember that you and your partner are on the same team. Rah-rah.
- Remember that some things will happen that are out of your control or the control of your adoption professional. For example, sometimes moms do have a change of mind and heart, despite their "best laid plans," when it comes to placing their child for adoption. This isn't anyone's fault. A mother has every right to parent her child. Adoption is a risky, rough journey for many, and you just have to hang on and see what happens. (I know. Comforting, Rach. Real comforting.)

No one enjoys hang ups, time outs, and bumps in the road. Have your favorite wine and chocolate on standby. You WILL need it.

Flyin' Solo

'm often asked about independent adoptions, which is when a prospective adoptive person or couple advertises themselves to secure a placement. Usually this is done to avoid big agency fees (advertising, placement, etc.). The hopeful parent advertises on paper (pass along cards, flyers, mini profile books left at crisis pregnancy centers and with hospital social workers) and electronically (ads on social media, public adoption profile pages, websites that host adoption profiles, etc.).

Yes, successful matches and placements happen via the "flyin' solo" method, but I personally wasn't comfortable going this route. After adopting four times using a small, ethical adoption agency, let me explain to you why we made the choice we did, to use an agency, versus going out on our own.

1: An agency provides counseling to the expectant mom (or connects the mom to a counselor).

This is so important. An ethical counselor will help the mom explore her options and consider the pros and cons of parenting versus placing. Now, many argue (and I can see why) that an agency providing counseling is going to be bias toward adoption. But to counter that argument, an adoption agency understands adoption (including the long-term effects) better than many counselors. What it comes down to for us, is choosing ethical agencies who support moms no matter what they choose: to place or parent.

2: I wasn't willing to put my personal information, including photos, into public spaces.

There are definite safety concerns when you put your personal information "out there" for anyone to see and use. It is so incredibly easy to find out more information about someone, especially the way social media algorithms work, based on just a tidbit of information. I was unwilling to share photos of our home, our current children, our hometown, etc., risking having our pictures stolen (and used inappropriately, which happens far too often), our information available to anyone, or worse, being scammed. See next point.

3: I didn't want to constantly question if I was dealing with a scammer.

An agency helps determine if an expectant mother is pregnant, is considering adoption, and truly needs assistance. I didn't want to make those calls or end up on a nightly news special, ugly crying. It's unfortunate that so many scams happen, and hopeful parents are taken advantage of, sometimes draining their bank accounts. Utilizing an agency and attorney helped us feel more secure.

4: It's not ethical for a hopeful parent to play dual roles.

The main problem with flyin' solo is that the hopeful parent becomes the expectant parent's social worker, which is, of course, unethical. You can't be the one hoping and praying for a baby while offering unbiased advice and guidance to the expectant mother. It's not good for you, and it's not good for her. I know many expectant and hopeful parents grow very close during the pregnancy, which has its pros and cons. But the bottom line is that there is no way a hopeful parent can be fair when she is thrust into the position of social worker.

I know people who have had fairly successful independent adoptions. And I certainly understand why any person doesn't (and can't) hand over $10,000 plus to an adoption agency. However, for the reasons listed above, we went the agency route, successfully and happily.

Pop Quiz

I f you get on any online adoption support page, you'll see posts heavily sprinkled with adoption terminology. Some of this might make your head spin. So my gift to you right now is this: a glossary of terms. I know what you're thinking. *Rachel, you promised me no bolded vocabulary words and no textbook nonsense.* Ok, yes, I remember that, but trust me, though I won't be issuing you an exam, if you mess these terms up online, someone will call you on it and give you a verbal butt-whoppin'. Don't say I didn't warn you if you get lazy and skip over this chapter.

In no particular order, here's some terminology for the adoption in-crowd:

Birth Parent: Also known as a biological parent, a natural parent, a first parent, even a "tummy mummy,[12]" is the parent who conceived (mother and father) and gave birth to the child (mother). A birth parent is <u>not</u> someone who is considering adoption or has made an adoption plan. It is not appropriate to shorten birth mom to "BM" on social media or elsewhere. BM is an acronym for bowel movement. Have some respect, sister.

Expectant Parent: This is the preferred term describing a parent who is expecting a baby and is considering making an adoption plan for their child or has made an adoption plan for their child. (Any parent expecting a child, by birth or adoption, can also be considered an expectant parent.) A

---

12 From my understanding, the term "tummy mummy" comes from adoptee and parent-by-adoption Michelle Madrid-Branch who wrote the children's book *The Tummy Mummy*.

parent isn't a "birth parent" if and until they place their child for adoption. Online you'll see "EM" in reference to expectant moms.

Adoptee: An adopted person. Some adoptees say they "were adopted" (a past event) and some say they "are adopted" (continual).

Adoptive Parent: Also known as a parent (yep, just a parent!) who has adopted a child. I prefer to say parent-by-adoption when trying to clarify in certain situations. On social media, you'll see "AP" in reference to parents who have adopted their children.

Prospective/Hopeful/Waiting Adoptive Parent: Those waiting to adopt. Prospective adoptive parent is sometimes referred to as PAP. (If pap smear came to mind, you aren't alone.)

Failed Adoption: This term is used when parents made an adoption plan for their child (and selected a person or couple to adopt their child) but chose to parent instead of place the child. When the adoption plan is changed to a parenting plan, the person or couple hoping to adopt the child has experienced a failed adoption.

Termination of Parental Rights: This is known as TPR in the adoption community. This means the child's biological parent(s) have either voluntarily surrendered their rights to their biological child or their rights have been terminated through the legal system (which is the case in some foster care cases or in situations where the birth father is unknown or unnamed). TPR paperwork is sometimes referred to as "surrenders."

Placed: This term refers to the act of a biological parent voluntarily surrendering their child for adoption. This is the politically correct, current term used. However, sometimes birth parents and adoptees will talk about children being "put up" or "given up" for adoption.

Parented: This term refers to an expectant parent choosing to parent their child instead of place as planned.

Attachment Parenting: Also known as AP, attachment parenting is when parents use certain mindsets and techniques (for example, co-sleeping, nursing, baby-wearing) to help the baby attach securely to the parent. (More on why AP should be considered by parents who adopt in a later chapter.)

Primal Wound: The primal wound refers to the idea that child experiences a traumatic loss when separated from his or her biological parent.

The primal wound theory has been vehemently debated in the adoption community.[13]

Original Birth Certificate: Also known as the OBC, the original birth certificate is the one registered when the adoptee is born. This birth certificate is amended to state the names of the adoptive parent(s) once the baby has been legally adopted. Not all states allow adoptees access to their OBCs, but this is gradually (and rightfully, in my opinion) changing.

Finalization: This is the point in time in which the adoption becomes "final" in the eyes of the law. Finalization requirements and procedures vary by state.

Post-Placement: These refer to the required process in which the parent with a new adoptive placement demonstrates that the placement is a healthy situation. Usually the post-placement process includes visits from a social worker and paperwork. This paperwork is used at finalization to prove to a judge that the adoption is acceptable and should be legally approved.

Punitive Father Registry: The registry in which a natural father or an alleged natural father can file to be a potential father to a child.

Interstate Compact on Placement of Children: ICPC is when the state you are residing in and the state the baby (and/or biological parents) is from exchange a whole freaking lot of paperwork to make sure that everything is up to par with the adoption process and the parties involved.

Post-Adoption Depression: Also known as PAD. Post-Adoption Depression is surprising similar to Post-Partum Depression. Families who adopt may experience physical, emotional, spiritual, and financial issues as a result of the new child joining their family.[14]

Trying to Conceive: Also known as TTC. You'll see this in posts from people "feeling out" adoption as a family building-option. For example, "We've been TTC for six years with no success."

---

13 Nancy Verrier thoroughly explores the primal wound theory in her book *The Primal Wound: Understanding the Adopted Child* (2003).

14 For more on this, see *The Post-Adoption Blues: Overcoming the Unforeseen Challenges of Adoption* by Karen J. Foli and John R. Thompson (2004) and *Adoption Therapy: Perspectives from Clients and Clinicians on Processing and Healing Post-Adoption Issues* edited by Laura Dennis (2014).

Homestudy: This is the document that gives you a "pass" to adopt. It means you've been approved, officially, to pursue adopting. It reads much like a formal biography about your family. There is information about you physically, financially, socially. It might outline your parenting style, your family history, your marriage (if applicable), what type of adoption you are pursuing, and much more.

Acronyms for the In-Crowd (That's You, Girl)

Here are some acronyms you might want to familiarize yourself with if for nothing else than your own amusement:

PGOMLN: People Getting on My Last Nerve. This might refer to your social worker, your friends and family members, even your partner. Adoption is stressful. I recommend taking your rear to Costco to purchase several mega-packs of Puffs Plus and boxed wine. Consider it an investment, but don't try to submit it as an adoption expense to the IRS. You are asking to be audited.

INAD: I Need a Drink. A cry for help. Real friends will pony up.

ISTMOAT: I Spent Too Much on Amazon Today. May or may not have been items baby or adoption related. May have been a sudden urge to diffuse essential oils in your house to calm your nerves resulting in spending $123.76 on a diffuser and an organic "simma down now" oil blend. But hey, at least you earned free shipping. That means you *saved* money, right?

IHPAA: I Hate Pet Adoption Ads. Adopting a pet isn't the same as adopting a child. Not even freaking close. I'm convinced that this might be in the Bible.

EIHABBM: Everyone is Having a Baby But Me. You follow this up with INAD and ISTMOAT.

PWS: Pregnant Women Suck. Hey, it's ok to not be down with women rubbing their rounded middles as if it's a genie in a bottle situation. Blech. At least you can drink.

IWSTT: I Want Special Treatment Too. No one offers to rub your feet or get you some tacos at 10 p.m. But you are a Real Expecting Mom (a REM. More on that later).

BAFE: Babies Are Freaking Everywhere. And they all look completely adorable, just like the moms who are pushing the strollers with the poise (and lipstick and blinding white teeth and tans) of Miss America.

DWTHYSAHS: Don't Want to Hear Your Secondhand Adoption Horror Story. Your fourth cousin's step-mom's best friend's brother-in-law is in jail for arson, certainly related to the fact that he was adopted. No. Just no. INAD.

IHAHC: I Have Another Hand Cramp. Could be from getting finger-printed (again, because they lost the first set) or from the 1,462 documents you have to sign swearing you aren't crazy. Or it could be from the locks you had to put on every cabinet in your home. Or, it could be from the fifth check you wrote to your agency in two months. Possibilities!

Poop

I have your attention, don't I?

I'll keep this short and sweet.

When referring to a mom who is expecting a baby (with whom you are matched with), she is an expecting mom. Period. EM on social media is fine.

Do not, do not, do not refer to the EM you are matched with as "our birth mom" or "our expectant mom." Take the "our" out of your vocabulary. You do not own her. I know, you are trying to be endearing and inclusive, embracing this new season in life, but just don't. The baby, if he or she becomes yours, is the one who can refer to the birth mother with ownership: "my birth mom." Plus, "our birth mom" is just weird because she's not you and your partner's birth mom, and in fact, she's not a birth mom at all!

Remember, a birth mom is someone who has placed a child for adoption. A birth mom is not a woman who is expecting a baby and who has made an adoption plan for that baby.

Onto the poop part. Do not abbreviate birth mom to BM. Like ever. Don't be lazy. The least you can do is type out the words "birth mom." BM is an acronym for Bowel Movement. Gross.

I'm only trying to prevent you from getting a virtual beating on social media. The adoption community takes their terminology seriously. It's not about being PC, before you get your granny panties[15] in a wad about that. It's about being respectful, empathetic, and receptive.

Finally, though birth mom is the common term to describe a woman who has placed a baby for adoption, there are others: natural mother (which is commonly a legal term), biological mother (again, no acronyms, please!), first mother, tummy mummy/mommy, Mommy (insert first name).

I'm not here to tell you which one is right or wrong. I'm well aware that some of these make you squirm. And truly, how a child refers to his or her birth mother should be up to them. Of course, you as the parent guide the child. Just make sure you're open to the possibilities, allowing your child to freely express his or her emotions and understanding of the adoption, THEIR adoption.

So steer-clear of the toileting references. They're offensive. And they are certainly the opposite of wise.

---

15 No shame in my game. Wear big, comfortable underwear, or don't wear any. But please don't spend $15 on a lacy string that rubs your nethers all the live long day. I'm pretty sure your gyno would agree.

The Social Worker Wears a White Glove

The homestudy refers to a lengthy, detailed document outlining your readiness to adopt a child. It is as unintrusive as a pap smear.

Homestudies are completed by a social worker. Now, I know what your vision of a social worker is: a middle-aged woman who wears a business suit, reading glasses, and carries a clipboard. She has pursed lips and deadpan stare. She is punctual. She is the great Gatekeeper who stands between you and your future baby. There just might be a pointer in her back pocket.

I'm friends with a few social workers, and they are kind individuals who stepped into their jobs much like many teachers do: to make a difference in the lives of others. They work long, sporadic hours, are usually underpaid, and often go unappreciated, ending up long-forgotten by the individuals they lovingly serve. Like most teachers I know, social workers do what they do because they are passionate about the people and the purpose.

And here's the good news: they don't wear or own white gloves.

So take your chill pill[16] and read on.

---

16 Do not literally use pills as a means of regulating your adoption-induced emotions. I recommend cheese fries or funnel cakes instead. They are a highly nutritious. Also, I am not a doctor. Do not listen to me.

On Not Saving the Trees

Homestudies are not eco-friendly. There are stacks (yes, stacks) of paperwork to fill out. Much this paperwork will be repetitive and mind-numbing. Do you remember taking state required essay tests in school? Remember those hand cramps from spending hours gripping your number 2 pencil? Guess what, friend? That hand cramp is back! How nostalgic, right?

Common paperwork in the homestudy process:

- <u>Initial application</u>. This is a form outlining basics like your name, address, place of employment, list of character references, and general health and financial information. Plus, be ready to cut a check to the business as a "thank you for reading my paperwork to determine my future" gesture. (Typically once this is accepted, you will have to fill out a more detailed application.)
- <u>Background check forms</u>. No one wants to give a baby to an arsonist or drug addict.[17]
- <u>Questionnaires</u>. About you, your partner, your relationship, your health history, your predicted parenting style, your motivation to

---

17 I warned you about pills.

adopt.[18] These are often referred to as "self" and "couple" studies. (Yes, it's weird to be required to study yourself.)

- Proof. A fire escape plan, proof of medical and life insurance, and proof of employment.
- Pet records. Usually this means immunization records.
- Letters of reference. Usually required: character references (three to five) and sometimes a letter from your church leader (if religion is a requirement).
- Lots of papers to sign and date. These include the agency's fee schedule, grievance policy, etc.

Remember, I told you that you would experience hand cramps. Now stop jacking around and go sharpen some pencils.

---

18 Here's a story for ya. One agency's paperwork asked us to detail our "intimate life" as a couple. If I would have been wittier then and less scared of the entire adoption process, I would have provided a paragraph ripped right from a romance novel. Instead, I think I wrote "fine" or something similarly vague and prudish.

Law & Order: Special Adoption Unit (Dun Dun)

Y ou may wonder why it's necessary to be interviewed when you are often asked the same questions on forms. Agencies are looking for consistent responses and honesty from prospective parents. It's also the agency's way of practicing their due diligence. They want to make sure you are who you say you are and that you and your partner are on the same page. Since the agency serves as your representative and sometimes also for the baby and birth parents, they are responsible for making sure everything is on the "up and up."

During our first homestudy process, our social worker came to our home to interview us as a couple and then each of us individually. During my husband's interview, I went into our home office, laid across the floor, and pressed my ear into the crack between the door and the carpet. I gained absolutely nothing from doing that, except a carpet imprint on my cheek. (Lindsay, if you read this, I'm only mildly embarrassed by my actions.)

Do not sweat such interviews. You don't need to prepare for them in the way you would for a job interview. Just show up and be you.[19]

---

19 What if the social worker asks questions that make you squirm, such as questions about a criminal past, a tragic event in your life, or something similar? Just tell the truth, because the truth will become clear once your background checks arrive or your spouse gives away parts of your story during his/her interview. Once the social worker leaves, you can bust out your box-o-wine I told you to have on hand and chocolate chip cookies.

Martha Stewart Meets Bundle of Joy

E xperienced parents-by-adoption will tell you that the home inspection is no big deal. I know you have heard this, but you won't listen. You will clean out your sock drawer, alphabetize your spices, bleach your shower until you are chemical-drunk, spend weeks choosing just the right apple pie scented candle, redecorate your living room (with plenty of framed photos of you snuggling your niece and nephew with a glorious sunset in the background), and you will baby proof the house to the extreme.[20]

I get it. You want to make a good impression. You want your home to say, "I'm ready to house a precious human child with my cleanliness, warmth, and lovely décor."[21]

If you can, obtain a list of requirements before your social worker visits. You will feel more at-ease if you are prepared.

Generally, it is a good idea to:

---

20 Unless you want to laugh at your social worker who spends five minutes in your bathroom trying to get the toilet seat unlocked, I recommend just making sure your home is pleasant enough and basically safe. It's also not a good idea to laugh at your social worker.

21 I hate to tell you, but your baby will not care a bit about your choice in throw pillows. But hey, knock yourself out, girl. Distraction and attention to detail can be a beautiful thing.

- Place all chemicals and medications in locked, high cabinets.
- Have working fire and carbon dioxide detectors and alarms, particularly in all the main living areas and in all bedrooms.
- Have a fire extinguisher. Be sure any lighters and matches are in a safe place.
- Make sure any pools, hot tubs, and guns are secure (and legal!).
- Put locks and guards on outlets, lower cabinets, and on door knobs. Have baby gates at the top and bottom of stairs. It's also a good idea to have a lock on your oven door and put kid-safety items over the oven knobs if they are on the front of the oven.
- Make sure your hot water heater is set at a safe temperature.
- Fix any glaringly obvious safety issues: a broken spindle on a staircase, for example, or a rickety board on the back deck.
- Clean out your future child's bedroom and have it ready to show your worker.

The goal is not to have a perfect house that would earn you a high-five from Martha Stewart. The social worker is trying to make sure your home is safe, clean, and healthy for a child.

Misc. Etc.

Here are a few more things you need to be aware of:

- Much of the homestudy process is in your hands. How quickly you have a homestudy in-hand depends on your ability to fill out the paperwork and your openness to the availability of the social worker (for the home inspection and interviews). The paperwork isn't rocket science.[22] It's just time consuming and cumbersome.
- Your social worker doesn't work 24/7/365. Unless you have a real emergency (like a baby just dropped from the sky into your lap on a Saturday night), do not e-mail your social worker a question about your paperwork, only to text her from your spouse's phone (sneak attack/test) as you are leaving the social worker a voicemail from your phone. Don't be annoying.
- That said, being persistence is OK. This is *your* homestudy and *your* adoption journey. Speak up if your social worker isn't a good match for you (personality wise) or if he or she isn't doing a good job. If your needs aren't met as expected and promised, follow the grievance procedure.

---

22 Is rocket science literally science that involves rockets? I have no idea. I failed chemistry in high school and barely passed biology in college; science isn't my thing.

- Don't become completely consumed by the homestudy process. Adoption is a life-long journey, not a season to get through as quickly as possible. Don't neglect your partner, your current children, your parents, your friends, or your job responsibilities. You still have a life to live.
- Ask your social worker questions, share your concerns, and ask for resources. Part of your social worker's job is to do these things.

And remember, distraction is an art. Take a break from filling out the paperwork and read the latest smutty celeb gossip, have coffee with a friend, or rage clean. We all need vacas from reality sometimes.

Creating Your Adoption Profile Book: Round One

T he first thing you will think when you sit down to do your profile book is, "Wow. I suck." Then you will gradually get more excited and then completely obsessed. You will be blurry-eyed, staring at your computer screen for hours, with a cramp in your back and a mug of cold coffee in your hand. You will type photo captions. And then you will delete them. Then you will retype what you typed twenty minutes ago. Then you will delete it again. You will agonize over every single word. You will write "Dear Expectant Mother" only to delete it and write, "Hi, friend!!!" only to delete two of the three exclamation points, only to add them back in, plus a few more, only to delete the entire line because you know how corny writing, "Dear friend!!!!" to someone you've never met sounds. You might try "Dearest Lady" as if you are inviting royalty over for afternoon tea (What are you? British?) or something equally as weird.

You will then devote no fewer than four entire pages of your profile book to your two dogs. I mean, if you can care for dogs, you can care for a kid, right? WRONG! You realize how ridiculous it is, how you appear to be a crazy dog lady, and you will delete these pages only to feel guilty that you minimized the importance of your fur-babies who are lovingly curled up around your feet as you work.

You will then focus on talking about yourself. Unless you are a narcissist, this will be incredibly challenging for you. All the sudden your job sounds so ordinary. Your hobbies? Vanilla. The low-fat version. Your personality? Bore-Fest. You realize you haven't done anything on your bucket list, you loathe your boss and want to quit your job and instead become someone who gets paid to look at Pinterest all day.[23]

Instead of continuing to attempt to write about yourself, you write a paragraph on why you are choosing adoption. Before you know it, you are sobbing, snot running down your face, as you recall all the infertility treatments you've been through. You wipe your snot on your oversized tee, because getting up to find a tissue would make you lose your momentum. You decide that to cheer yourself up, you will try to find some pictures demonstrating to an expectant mother how mom-worthy you are. You find some saved images on your computer of you cuddling your nieces and nephews. This only makes you more depressed, because your nieces and nephews are now in middle school and you are still without a little bundle of joy. You decide to abandon that task, get yourself some sort of 1000 calorie-per-half-cup of chocolate ice cream from the freezer that you hid from your husband and start noshing on it while you browse baby name websites.

Four hours later, you realize you have won an award! That is, the Most Pathetic Adoption Profile Book Ever award.

Until...it dawns on you to look at some examples from others. BAD IDEA, SISTER! The online examples are too damn perfect! They look like Pottery-Barn-meets-J-Crew catalogs! These other couples have it going on! I mean, one owns a vacation home in Hawaii! Ha-freaking-waii. Another speaks four languages, spends weekends volunteering for Habitat for Humanity, and only buys clothing that is fair-trade-organic-dye-free. That woman's socks cost more than half your wardrobe!

You decide, once again, that you suck. You wipe the chocolate ice cream residue on your pajama pants and shut your laptop down. Screw it. You'll just remain childless!

---

23 If you somehow find that this is a for-realz job, can you please e-mail me ASAP?

Creating Your Adoption Profile Book: Round Two

First, you don't suck. You don't. Most couples and singles waiting to adopt are ordinary people with a common dream: to become a mom or dad. They live in ordinary places, work ordinary jobs, and have ordinary hobbies.

Get a list of your agency's profile book requirements. Read them over carefully, and ask your social worker questions. Ask to see some samples, if possible, from your agency.

I want you to work on your profile book with this mindset: Be yourself. Say it aloud. I mean it. Do it! "BE MYSELF."

The thing is, you owe expectant parents the truth, no matter how boring, unimpressive, or flawed you think you are. You also never know what an expectant parent may connect with in your book. It could be your love of pets, your favorite baseball team, your profession, your home. It could be the tone in which you present yourself in your book: funny, serious, quirky. It might be your priorities, your faith, or your photographs taken from all the places you've traveled.

Should you hire a professional to design your profile book for you, especially if you are a person who struggles with writing and graphic design? Possibly. Professional profile creation services can be expensive, but you might choose to build that service into your adoption budget.

If you are determined to create your book yourself, I recommend purchasing and reading Madeleine Melcher's book *How to Create a Successful Adoption Portfolio: Easy Steps to Help You Produce the Best*

Adoption Profile and Prospective Birthparent Letter and reviewing Positive Adoption Language (PAL) online. This is a list of appropriate terms used in the adoption community. After you've read Madeleine's book and review PAL, start drafting your profile book.

Creating Your Adoption Profile Book: Third Time's a Charm

A fter you've created a draft of your book, please have someone with an affinity for grammar, punctuation, and spelling look over your book for you. Offer them something deliciously sugary in exchange for their time and energy. In addition, when reviewing your book, ask yourself:

- Have I been authentic throughout?
- Have I offered significant detail to give any viewers true insight into who I am?
- Have I included photos that illustrate who I am and what I enjoy?
- Are the photos clear and appropriate? (Please, please do not make your cover photo, or any photo in your book for that matter, a bathroom mirror selfie. You are not nineteen and at the club. Have some professional photos taken if need be.)
- Have I kept very personal details private until an organic relationship can be formed? (Details like the exact town I live in, the company I work for, my last name, etc.)
- Have I refrained from any adoption language that isn't encouraged by the Positive Adoption Language list?
- Have I refrained from telling a "sob story" that will put guilt upon the expectant mother, while being transparent about why I'm choosing adoption and my journey to that choice?

- Have I made promises that I intend to keep in terms of an ongoing relationship?
- Is this book something I'm proud to put my name on?
- Is this book something that I'm willing to let my future children see, knowing that I presented my authentic self?

Once you are satisfied with your honest, heartfelt, aesthetically pleasing book, it's ready! Cheers!

The Checklist

The two worst parts of the adoption journey for me was the waiting (always the waiting) and the checklist.

In case you aren't there yet, the checklist is what your adoption professional hands you and says, "Tell us what situations you are open to." I refer to it as the "dreaded" checklist, because, well, I dread it.

As you glance over the document, likely a few pages in length, you begin to feel pretty darn dirty, like you've just stolen $100 from your grandma's purse, spent it on prostitute-worthy cosmetics, and then denied knowledge of where the money went when your grandma asks. It's that bad. Prepare thyself.

What is the point of the checklist? The professional wants to know which situations you would consider in terms of openness in the relationship, the expectant mother and father's health history, exposure to things like drugs and alcohol, expectant parent expenses, etc.

What I want you to know is that behind this checklist are *people*: the biological parents and the child.

I don't say this to guilt you into saying "yes." But I want you to make every single decision out of education, not out of ignorance. Do your research. Don't swiftly fill out the checklist so you can "get a move on" (that's called baby hunger, and you need to calm down). Talk to medical professionals about mental illness and drug exposure. Talk to adoptees about their experiences with openness with their birth families (or lack thereof). Talk to other parents-by-adoption about their reasoning behind the openness they chose.

If you aren't certain what to check, there's usually a "will consider" or "maybe" column, which can be your best friend. It's OK, even wise, to take each situation into consideration on a case-by-case basis. And it's not a "situation" or a "case" in all actuality. It's people, your fellow human beings, and their future (and your future too). In doing so, you need to remember that you have the right and responsibility to say no if a possible adoption isn't right for you and your family.

You aren't ordering up a sandwich, putting together a show-stopping outfit, or throwing together the coolest mix-tape ever. You are adopting a human. Take the checklist seriously. Naturally, celebrate the completion of the checklist with chocolate covered strawberries, because, carbs.

It Takes Two

There are many special situations in adoption. Though this discussion of birth fathers shouldn't be a special situation, it often is. In many states, the birth father's rights and responsibilities aren't the same as the birth mother's. Because of this, adoptions can get legally and ethically complicated.

There are cases where the birth mother might be married to a man who isn't the child's birth father. There are cases where the birth mother lies about who the birth father is or doesn't know who he is. There are cases where the expectant mother is trying to stay as far away as possible from the expectant father so that he doesn't interfere with the adoption plan. Perhaps the birth father is much older or much younger than the birth mother, and she is ashamed of this fact. Maybe the birth father is abusive.

Please remember that there are two sides to every story. The birth father may or may not be the person he's been painted as by the birth mother or by anyone else. He should be given the benefit of the doubt and not vilified. Remember that no matter what, if the placement happens, he is your child's birth father, and talking negatively about him (sometimes unfounded) isn't going to bode well for your relationship with your child.

In any case, it's wise of any parent to have a "quad A" (AAAA) attorney handling the father's rights, preferably someone who is ethical and experienced. The most ideal of adoptions means each party (parents who hope to adopt and the biological parents) have separate and equally-as-qualified legal representation.

Open Adoption

When we were first waiting to adopt, we swiftly checked the semi open adoption box. It seemed like a happy middle ground, a perfect compromise. However, the more we learned about open adoption, by reading *The Open Adoption Experience* (Lois Ruskai Melina and Sharon Kaplan Roszia, 1993) and more recently, *The Open-Hearted Way to Open Adoption* (Lori Holden with Crystal Hass, 2015) and with time and experience, we have fully embraced open adoption.

Each open adoption is different. Some involve a lot of contact and face-to-face visits, while others involve just a once-a-year visit. Some involve video chat sessions, texts, e-mails, and phone calls. Some involve the adoption agency or attorney acting as a "middle man." Some adoptions begin open and move toward more of a closed adoption, while some go the opposite way, while some are strong and steady.

As with any relationship, it's healthy to allow it to build organically over time. Trust, respect, and love grow in layers over many seasons and experiences. Throwing open the door to open adoption in the hopes of securing a faster match and placement, doing it because your agency demands it, or agreeing to it for only a period of time (say until finalization) in an attempt to appease the child's birth parents is not ideal or appropriate.

I am asked a lot about our open adoptions. We're either met with awe and appreciation or doubt and discouragement. Open adoption is a fairly new phenomenon, one that is gaining popularity. Here are some questions you may have about open adoption[24]:

Isn't open adoption like sharing or co-parenting the child with the birth parents? Well, sort of. I mean, the birth parents had the child first. But we are parenting the child now. The visits, the communication, the exchange of information are all for the benefit of the adoptee. In a way, we do share the child: we share love for the child and with the child, we share a vested interest in how the child does in life, we care about what happens to the child. We, as the parents, have the job and the honor of raising the child, of making the day-to-day parenting decisions, of being responsible for the child's safety and well-being, of nurturing the child to become a successful adult. Do we co-parent? Not in a traditional sense, like a divorced couple who co-parents a child. But in a non-traditional sense? Yes. Because only certain parents can provide certain things for the child. If the child has a question about the circumstances of his or her placement, that information coming from a birth parent, if possible, would be more comprehensive than it coming second-hand from the parent who has adopted the child.

Won't the kids be confused? No. My kids aren't confused at all. Our family "orchard" (as we call it) is no different, really, than a step-family, a child raised by grandparents, a child with two moms or two dads. The idea of a traditional family with a traditional family "tree," seems to be less and less the norm in society. Kids are adaptable. They do learn, quickly, what their normal is, as long as there is honesty.

But what do the kids call their birth parents? To each his or her own on this one! Some birth parents preferred to be referred to as birth parent, natural parent, first parent, tummy mummy[25], or biological parent. When being addressed by the family, some use first names, some use "aunt" or "uncle," some use a special name. What the birth parent is called by the child is personal and might change over time. I read several years ago

---

24 I write about open adoption a lot on my blog, whitesugarbrownsugar.com. I hope you'll stop by!

25 "Tummy mummy," to my understanding, was coined by adoptee and mom-by-adoption Michelle Madrid-Branch, in her children's book.

that a parent shouldn't overreact or aggressively correct the name the adoptee choses to refer to his or her biological parents, unless that name is inaccurate. The child will be processing his or her adoption story over a lifetime, so terminology and names may naturally change throughout the years.

What about boundaries, though? When you agree to a match or a placement, it's crucial that you set up some sort of expectations in terms of the openness in the adoption. And please, please don't make promises that are set to dictate the adoption for the long-term. Your child should have a say-so in the openness of the adoption when he or she is old enough; therefore, it's impossible to promise what will happen in terms of visits and communication over the course of the next eighteen years. A good rule of thumb is to set up expectations for the next six months, and then re-evaluate after that.

What parents-by-adoption need to know is that open adoption isn't a competition. It isn't necessary for all of the child's parents (whether they are by adoption or by birth) to fend for a gold medal that doesn't exist. I encourage parents to intentionally allow the child to feel comfortable expressing his or her thoughts about adoption, about birth parents, and about the open adoption relationship, not putting words in the child's mouth, influencing the child to feel a certain way, and not put pressure on the child to choose. It's unhealthy[26], and it's completely unnecessary.

---

26 What is healthy? CARBS! What is with these women going on no-carb diets? You may get five pounds lighter, but you'll also become a hangry B that no one wants to be friends with. You may have come to this book seeking adoption advice, but I'm giving you nutritional advice too: eat the carbs.

Toxic Relationships

Sometimes it's not healthy or appropriate to have an open adoption or a current relationship with the child's biological parents. Perhaps this is because of choices or circumstances that the birth parents are in such as an abusive relationship, drug abuse, or refusing to acknowledge and respect the child's parents in their role.

Don't go from sixty to zero. Meaning, don't have a ridiculous policy like "one strike and you're out" toward the biological parents. Everyone needs grace, second chances, space, and time. Closing an adoption upon the first "infraction" isn't cool. There should be steps taken to rectify relationships, particularly when they are new relationships. Keep your adoption professional involved to help everyone navigate murky waters.

On the other hand, giving chance after chance despite broken promises and boundary-pushing is naïve and can be detrimental to the child. If expectations have been clearly established and communicated, if the involvement of a professional hasn't helped, and if the relationship seems to be one-sided, it's time to take a break. No need for drastic measures where you swear off all contact forever. However, I have met many parents who continue to push for openness, despite obvious inappropriate choices by the child's birth parents, out of guilt or obligation.

As a parent to a young child, you have the job of protecting your child, establishing boundaries, and reasonably expecting those to be met. Parenting is certainly not always easy; however, you have been chosen to parent your child. Do your job.

Transracial Adoption

have a whole lot to say on this topic. It's the primary focus on my blog, in many of my articles, and media appearances. It's so important that I wrote an entire book about it called *Come Rain or Come Shine: A White Parent's Guide to Adopting and Parenting Black Children*.

Here's what you need to know in a very small nutshell:

- Transracial adoption isn't for everyone. And that is OK.
- Love isn't enough to raise a child who doesn't racially match you. Love is a fantastic foundation, but it isn't all the child will need.
- Transracial adoptees' needs are different from the needs of adoptees who racially match their parents; therefore, the whole color-blind approach isn't going to fly. Race should be celebrated and acknowledged, not ignored.
- Transracial adoption might require you to make a lot of changes in your life, including where you live, where your child will go to school, where you work, who you hang around with, your relationships with family and friends, what you read and listen to.
- Transracial adoption isn't something to be taken or entered into lightly.
- Transracial adoption shouldn't be chosen because it seems cool or trendy, because you think bi-racial babies are cute, because a celebrity adopted a child from China, or because you've just always wanted to adopt transracially. Transracial adoption means

bringing a child, a human being, into your home who will require much of you.

- Transracial parenting should never be done in isolation. This is why you need to live and work in a diverse community, why your child might benefit from a same-race mentor, why you'll need help with your child's hair and skin-care, and many more. It does take a village, and if you aren't comfortable with village-parenting, transracial adoption may not be for you.
- Transracial adoption means that your child's adoption will be obvious. You will be confronted more often than a same-race family about adoption and race.
- A child of color is a child of color. Some families go into adoption saying they will adopt a bi-racial child but not a "full Black" child, for example. This is completely ridiculous, in my humble opinion.
- A child won't be a baby forever. Parents who choose to adopt transracially need to be in it for the long-haul and understand the realities people of color face every day.
- Adopting transracially means that a prior same-race family becomes a multi-racial, multi-cultural family.

My first book discusses transracial adoption extensively and includes many resources, lists, stories, and discussion points, as well as ample research. If you are considering transracial adoption, you can get my book in paperback or as an e-book on Amazon.

Special Needs

My sweet godson is a little boy with extensive special needs. He was adopted when he was several months old, and being close to the family has taught me a lot about special needs adoption. Like transracial adoption, there are things to consider:

- Special needs adoption isn't for everyone. That is OK.
- "Special needs" includes a wide range. Many families decide which special needs they are open to and which they aren't; some agencies allow families to choose levels of special needs ranging from mild to extensive.
- Families need to be very honest with themselves about their motivation to adopt a child with special needs, as well as their resources. Do they have support? Are they able to take on a child's needs? Do they have the financial resources? Are they willing to move, if necessary, to a better school district or to a town that's located closer to the medical facilities that will help their child?
- What if the special needs child has more extensive needs than previously thought? Is the family committed no matter what?
- The parent must be willing to relentlessly advocate for their child's rights, making sure the child's needs are met.
- Not all parents intend to adopt a child with special needs, but sometimes the child they are matched with is born with or later develops special needs.

Before you begin the journey to adopt a child with special needs or are open to the possibility, meet with other families who have gone before you. Ask questions. Listen and learn. Remember that each child and each experience is different, but know that having a support system in place and a commitment to education, you're on the right track.

Multiples

ultiples. This usually evokes one of two responses: excitement ("I've always wanted twins!") or horror ("I cannot imagine!"). No matter which camp you fall into, multiples are viewed as a novelty (thank you, TLC). Again, it's OK to have a preference and to make that known to your social worker. A few things to consider:

- Do you have space for multiples?
- Do you have the finances to care for multiples?
- Do you have the family support to parent multiples?
- Are you prepared to be matched with a mom having multiples knowing that doing so means agreeing to a higher-risk pregnancy with potential medical complications?

And of course, ask yourself? : *Do I have a Costco membership?* If not, get one. They sell wine in fridge-friendly boxes and mega packs of diapers and wipes.

Stamp of Approval

Τ his chapter is short and sweet. Because you've been reading a lot. It's time to feel that you've accomplished something in your life. So read this chapter, and there you go. Completion.

Your social worker sends you a copy of the homestudy. Now, hold your horses, sister. Before you sign off on it, giddy with excitement and nervousness, go over the homestudy, in detail, and make sure there are no errors or misinformation. This document is uber-important: judges, attorneys, social workers, and guardian ad litems may read it. Get out the magnifying glass/fine-tooth comb and give it a few good reads; have your partner do the same. Notify your social worker of any issues: nicely.

Now it's time to celebrate! Pop open the champagne, talk about baby names, and knit some booties[27], because honey, you are now a waiting parent-to-be!

---

27 Do people actually knit booties these days? I'm sure someone on Etsy does!

Get Out the Megaphone & Get Ready for the Responses

S o you've made your plans. You've filled out all the paperwork. The homestudy is approved. You've submitted a profile book (after much agony over the wall color of your living room, where you opt to vacation, and the size of your husband's nose) and filled out the check-list. Now you are just waiting for THE call that will make you a mommy.

How do you share the news with family and friends? Can you just casually work adopting into a conversation? Like, "Hey, Aunt Josie. Yes, isn't this weather fantastic? I really enjoyed my three mile walk the other day. Work is going OK. My boss is being a pill, as usual, but I'm hopefully up for a promotion next month. Oh yes, and I'm adopting a baby. Did you see that hideous dress Kate Hudson wore to the Oscars? She has a bangin' body, so what was she thinking showing up in a $12,000 sequined tent? Great chat! Buh-bye!"

As you prepare to announce your someday-baby, you're probably feeling a slew of emotions: intimidation, anticipation, anxiety, skepticism, optimism. This is normal.

Some ways to announce your plans to adopt:

- Send out photo announcements.
- Start a rumor about yourself.
- Send a group text.
- Hire a sky-writer.
- Post an announcement on Facebook.

- Wear an "I'm paperwork pregnant"[28] t-shirt every day until everyone gets the message.

Be prepared. The moment you announce you are adopting, you will inevitably be met with some inappropriate questions and comments and "concerns." Some will present themselves passive-aggressively. Some will be sweetly ignorant. Others will use all the wrong words, asking at the perfectly worst time (say, over Thanksgiving dinner with thirty of your nearest-and-dearest staring blankly at you, waiting for your response…which may or may not have actually happened to me).

Here's a sampling of what may be thrust upon you. Don't shoot the messenger. I'm only looking out for your best interest here:

- <u>Questions about who is the infertile one</u>. Because laying blame is always healthy. Now, pass the mashed potatoes!
- <u>Questions about your sex life</u>. What positions have you tried? Maybe you just need to relax a little and let it happen. Don't forget about the aforementioned vegan lasagna. Yum, yum! Have you taken herbal supplements? Bisiting a chiropractor?
- <u>Questions about your ability to make decisions</u>. Don't you know that adopted kids have issues? Are you sure you want to be open to a child of any race? Why are you NOT open to a child of any race? Seriously, you're going to adopt a child from your own country when there are lots of little Chinese babies who need forever families? Have you tried having your "own" kids? Why didn't that work out?[29]
- <u>Questions about you're your finances</u>. Can you afford to adopt? Isn't it really expensive? You should definitely fundraise. Here are some tacky suggestions and a reference to buying a baby.

Announcing your plans to adopt, the "big reveal," can certainly be anxiety-inducing and simultaneously exciting. Brace yourself. The questions will come, often in the form of preconceived notions. Yes, this can be

---

28 I hate the term "paperwork pregnant." So weird. But hey, it's your t-shirt, honey.
29 Vicious cycle of interrogation.

hurtful, frustrating, and disappointing, particularly when these come from your nearest-and-dearest. More on this in the next chapter.

This journey is not for the faint at heart. But you probably figured that out by now.

Family Really is Like Chocolate: Mostly Sweet with a Few Nuts

Whether you have already revealed your decision to family members or you are simply considering doing so (and how), here are some helpful tips:

1: <u>Provide resources.</u> To deliver big news without anything to help family members process your choice can naturally be overwhelming for family. After all, it's likely they, like most of the general public, know very little information about adoption besides the inaccuracies they've likely seen in the media and in entertainment (such as in films and made-for-TV movies). I highly recommend *In On It: What Adoptive Parents Would Like You To Know About Adoption* (Elisabeth O'Toole, 2010) and *Adoption Is a Family Affair: What Relatives and Friends Must Know* (Patricia Irwin Johnston, 2012).

2: <u>Be open to further discussion.</u> Encourage your family members to share their concerns and questions with you. Be committed to listening and responding in love and education. Remember, these individuals have been your primary support system since you were young, so you can rely on one another while you navigate the adoption process.

3: <u>Include family members.</u> Whether you are putting together a nursery for the child you will adopt, shopping for baby clothing, or researching vaccines and parenting styles, invite family members

to participate.[30] This helps everyone build excitement and anticipation for the new arrival!

4: <u>Forgive, forgive, forgive.</u> Your family members will not always use
the right adoption terminology. They won't always understand
your choices. They may say the wrong things at the wrong times.
But keep in mind, they are learning and growing alongside you:
at their own pace. Gently correct, continue to provide resources,
and forgive freely.

5: <u>Don't forget about the after.</u> Even after you adopt, your family and
friends may have questions. Don't hesitate to occasionally send an
awesome article their way, especially if a recent conversation has
motivated you to dig deeper, learn more, and share that education with those who love your family.

6: <u>Have boundaries.</u> If a family member or friend is unwilling to
budge in terms of your child and his or her well-being, you have
to make some tough calls. This might be a racist uncle, an unsup-
portive sister, etc. These are not EASY calls to make, but they are
necessary. Your allegiance is to your child and your partner; everyone else is secondary.

Keep in mind, your family members need time, love, patience, and education in order to arrive where you are: accepting, excited, and prepared. It's
not always easy to wait for loved ones to catch up to you, but when they
do, it will be well worth it!

---

30 Caveat: QUALIFIED family members. Like not ones who are annoying, know-it-all, or
believe in tiny houses (because I cannot even deal with tiny house living as the cool new
thing. Trust me. As a mom, you will get touched out and want personal space, which will
only happen if you are a few hundred feet, at least, away from your partner and child).

Ready, Set, Wait!

Waiting sucks.[31]
You will be fed all sorts of clichés and questions and biblical references while waiting to adopt. As a result of the culmination of these, you want to scream and throw breakables (like vases, if you're the fancy type who owns such valuables) because it looks so dramatic and stress-relieving in the movies. Do not do this. You do not want to be hotlined by your neighbors and lose your chance to adopt because you are deemed crazy. You may also want to eat endless tubes of raw cookie dough. This is a perfectly understandable response. I have never, ever gotten sick from eating raw cookie dough.[32]

Let's review some things you might hear while waiting (because you aren't tired of hearing them, right?):

- Patience is a virtue.
- Heard anything yet?
- God's plan is at work.

---

31 "Sucks" is an inappropriate word my mother never let me use growing up. It was made popular by *The Simpsons*, a show I wasn't allowed to watch and have still never watched to this day, because I'm feeling Old Testament and honoring my mother.

32 I'm not a doctor, nurse, weight-loss coach, or dietician. But I am a type 1 diabetic who knows all too well how temporarily happy raw cookie dough can make one feel. Just be prepared for the possible consequences of doing so, including an upset stomach, a blood sugar spike, and a sugar-rush headache that only goes away from a four hour nap. Oh yes, and the weight gain…

- Your day is coming!
- Heard anything yet?
- What if the baby's real mom uses drugs while pregnant?
- I bet you'll get pregnant now what you've decided to adopt!
- Heard anything yet?
- You know, your kid might have a lot of problems…
- You are so lucky! You get to become a mommy without the labor pains, weight gain, or stretch marks!
- Any day now, right?
- So cool that you are adopting! I adopted a puppy last year!
- Heard anything yet?
- Isn't adoption really expensive?
- Do you get to pick out your baby?
- Patience produces character.
- Aren't you scared the baby's real parents will try to take him back?
- Do twins cost the same amount as a single baby?
- You aren't going to adopt a Black baby…are you?
- Are you going to get one of those cute little mixed babies? They are the CUTEST! Just the CUTEST!

See? You are already having so much fun! It's like your celebrity being grilled by paparazzi! *Over here, darling! Who designed your dress? Did you drop five pounds?*

Before you go ballistic, take a deep breath. I know, it sounds cliché, but do it. That's it. Now, here are some practical (and wise) ways to deal with waiting for your child:

- <u>Get educated on adoption and the specific type of adoption you are pursuing (such as the placement of a special needs child or adopting transracially)</u>. Read every book you can get your hands on. Articles, blog posts, films, and online communities can also be helpful. Note that what you read is never adoption gospel (the be-all, end-all to all-things-adoption), but various viewpoints can be incredibly helpful.
- <u>Take up a new hobby or take a class, something that brings you enjoyment and preferably, relaxation</u>. You do not, I repeat, do

not need more anxiety right now. In fact, it's about time you stop white-knuckling this book. (It's not a textbook, honey. There's no test at the end.) New hobbies might include photography or knitting[33]. Take a yoga or painting class. Join a roller derby team, which would be really badass.

- Journal. This might mean writing letters to your future child, recording your joys and concerns as you wait to adopt, doodling your feelings, or ranting about all those baby shower invitations stacking up on your counter. (Because everyone and her sister is pregnant right now, probably with adorable twins). Writing is a healthy form of reflection and release. I would know.
- Exercise. There are so many benefits to breaking a sweat. These include maintaining or losing weight, building strength and endurance, sleeping better, and releasing feel-good hormones called endorphins. Try exercising outdoors (the sunshine and fresh air will do you some good). Choose workouts that you enjoy and that you can commit to long-term. These need not be whatever is "in" right now or anything overly strenuous.
- Date your partner. Do not neglect your romantic relationship, and don't forget to have fun and enjoy the person you love! Date nights are great, but so are vacations or staycations. Include your partner in your new hobby or activity. Take this calmer season of your life as an opportunity to create a more adventurous "intimate" life that you can then outline in your next homestudy. If you should be so lucky (as I was!).
- Have fun with friends. The girlfriends who have been with you for years want to support you as you wait for your child. Don't check out on these gal-pals just because you are contemplating drowning yourself in a gallon of high-fructose corn syrup laden ice cream.

---

33 Remember, we discussed knitting booties earlier?

Desperate Times Call for...

ow that you know what you might do while waiting, here are some things wise and witty ladies do *not* partake in while waiting:

- Call, e-mail, and text your social worker every twenty minutes asking if you've been chosen yet.
- Stalk the other waiting adoptive-parents-to-be on your agency's website to see who has been placed and who hasn't.
- Egg or TP the homes of the other waiting families.
- Look up exes on Facebook just to see if they married and went on to have beautiful babies.
- Obsessively read other people's online adoption profiles while mumbling bitchy thoughts about their hairstyles, pets, and favorite sports teams. Likewise, do not look at those who have HGTV worthy homes, yearly vacations to Cabo, and careers as world-renowned physicians (who naturally have defined jawlines, thick and beachy hair, and muscular arms) with disgust.[34]
- Watch adoption-themed reality shows or any Lifetime or Hallmark movies.
- Meander around the mall where you will inevitably be surrounded by mothers pushing strollers which carry pudgy, giggly babies

---

34 Green doesn't look good on you, honey. Jealousy is a beast. Send it on its way.

dressed in outfits nicer than you've ever owned and who appear to be auditioning for a magazine cover contest.

- Park in the "expecting mother" designated parking space and then give the sign the middle finger as you saunter in to buy groceries. And when I say "groceries," I mean tequila and Doritos.
- Get a tattoo that went out of style ten years ago, just because you are having a "screw it" kind of day and want to do something you consider to be rebellious.
- Start a stringent diet that involves no carbs, no gluten, no meat, no preservatives, and no alcohol. Get real, honey.
- Laugh like a Disney villain and tell all your friends with kids how sad you feel for them, then burst into tears because you know you are being a jerk.
- Take up a dangerous hobby or activity like motorcycle stunt riding, fire-sword swallowing, or poisonous snake hunting.
- Show up to your cousin's baby shower with a scowl on your face and proceed to loudly sigh every five seconds while, in intervals, shove massive bites of cake into your mouth.[35]
- Put your entire life on hold just to sit at the kitchen table and drum your fingers on its surface while you mentally curse all fertile women, adorable newborns, social workers, other adoptive couples, and Jennifer Lopez.[36]

---

35 Girlfriend, it is understandably difficult for many who are waiting to adopt to be emotional during and after another woman's baby shower. Should you find yourself inconsolable, it's ok to decline attending a shower. It's better not to attend than to attend and spoil someone else's joy (you know, rain on her proverbial parade). Approach the woman personally, explain that you are in a fragile emotional state and won't be able to attend, and hand her a nice gift. A great friend or family member will understand and offer you a hug rather than judgment.

36 How can she be so pretty? I mean really, why didn't God save a little bit for the rest of us?

Let's Compare Pregnancy and Adoption...You Know, Just for Fun!

f you've elected to share your happy news with the masses, or maybe just your parents, in-laws, and besties, you may be met with some well-meaning, completely ignorant pregnancy vs. adopting comparisons. Here are a few of them:

- "Lucky you! No stretch marks!" Let me tell you, I have stretch marks. They are from growing very quickly during puberty. They aren't pretty, but they are there. Lots of you dear readers who have never been pregnant may also have stretch marks.
- "You get to keep drinking alcohol!" Yep. And it's a definite perk. However, drink too much, and you might tipsy-text your social worker. Not cool.
- "At least you won't gain weight!" Newsflash: eating your emotions should be a disorder called, you guessed it, Eating Your Emotions. When you choose to adopt, you will do something obsessive and compulsive, like eating too much. (Remember, I told you to exercise!)
- "You'll probably get pregnant now that you've decided to adopt." I can't even deal with this one. I mean, does it happen to some couples? Sure. Is it common? Nope.
- "You can avoid all those weird pickle and ice cream cravings." Thanks for the "encouragement." Deep sigh.

- "No middle of the night peeing sessions!" Oh, there will be middle-of-the-night issues. It's called baby dreams and panic attacks. They are no fun.

Just know this: people mean well. They want to be supportive. But sometimes you will want to slap them with the burrito you are trying to devour. You aren't alone, friend. Arm yourself for the journey. Your favorite wine in one hand, this book in the other.

You are a Real Expecting Mom

R ead that title again, sister. You are a REAL EXPECTING mom. I cannot let you read on without really letting this point sink in, because it is so important that you understand that REAL means REAL. And here are some things REMs do:

- <u>They nest</u>. Nesting refers to the time when pregnant women are close to giving birth, and they frantically prepare for the baby. Some do so practically (wash baby's coming home outfit) and some do so neurotically (scrub the interior of their washing machine with a toothbrush). But hey, who am I to judge? What would help you feel prepared for your future baby? Set up the nursery? Shop for some baby basics? Whatever it is, do it, with reckless abandon. There's no better time than the present.[37]
- <u>They have a baby shower.</u> There is nothing wrong with desiring a baby shower when you are adopting. Now, you may have to ask for it, making it perfectly clear you are VERY interested. My advice is not to have a shower for the baby you are matched with; that is incredibly heart-risky and can be considered presumptuous.

---

37 I hate clichés. But as I write, they won't stop popping into my head. Popping…you know, like when people say pregnant women look "ready to pop"? I hate puns, too. And right now, you might hate pregnant women. Current pregnant women, thinking-about-getting pregnant women, oops-I'm-preggers-again (put that to the beat of the Britney Spears' song) women, I was pregnant twenty years ago women…

Register for lots of yellow and green and white things. And then enjoy your shower.[38]

- They keep it real. Ask any woman at the end of her pregnancy, and she's not in the "grin and bear it" mode. She's miserable and ready to roll. Likewise, you may be experiencing a myriad of emotions as a REM: anger, anticipation, jealousy, fear, confusion, joy, frustration, anticipation. It's healthy and normal to have real feelings.[39]

- They prepare a nursery. Having a nursery set up for your future child is therapeutic for many REMs. It's a place to arrange and plan, a place to pray and think, even a quiet sanctuary where you can cry. If anything, it's a place to put all your cool baby shower gifts.

- They enjoy attention and congratulations. It's OK to be excited about adopting, to tell people you are adopting, and to talk about adopting. Know, however, that when informing others you are adopting, you may very well be met with questions, comments, and concerns. Many adoptive-moms-to-be have had moments where they've been discouraged by the non-ideal responses from their nearest-and-dearest. (More on this later.) This is when you want to make sure you have your designated cookie dough shelf in your fridge, fully stocked of course.

- They research. Expecting moms know that there will be many upcoming decisions. Topics to research include vaccines, diapering, and feeding.[40] Find your child a pediatrician. Find out what your employer offers in terms of parental leave.

- They dream and plan. What would you like to name your future baby? What are some traditions you cannot wait to share with your child? Who do you want to hire to do a photo shoot with you and your child after he or she arrives?

---

38 And please, please have some alcohol at your baby shower! And if your mother-in-law doesn't approve, SPIKE THE PUNCH!

39 It's important, however, to deal with real feelings in a healthy way. This might include seeing a professional counselor, venting to a girlfriend, or seeking wisdom from an adoption support group.

40 Definitely, for your amusement, ask a social media parenting group what their stance is on vaccines (or diapering, or formula vs. breastmilk), then sit back with a glass of wine, and watch the imploding volcano of responses. You're welcome for the suggestion.

Thoughts that May Run through Your Head

While you are waiting for your baby, you will have no fewer than 1,000,000 colliding thoughts. Most are unfounded and honestly, a bit crazy. But they are normal. A few examples include:

- **What if don't bond with my child?** Bonding takes time. The "instant love" a lot of mommies boast about simply isn't the case for many moms. It's okay to take your time and let the bonding process happen organically.
- **What if I constantly compare my child to other children?** Most moms do this for a season or even a lifetime. But as you parent, you'll discover that no two kids are the same. And trust me, you will find your kid to be the most specialist special child who ever lived. You will oohhhh and ahhhh over every little thing he or she does. Your kid will rip the smelliest fart ever, and you will cheer like you're witnessing the winning touchdown at the Super Bowl.
- **What if the adoption involves some legal risk and I can't sleep for six months straight?** You will not sleep for six months straight anyway, because you will have a baby.
- **What if my family members don't embrace the child?** You are your child's advocate, and anyone who doesn't get on board will need to take a long walk off a...well, you get it.
- **Will I feel like my child's real mom?** Yes. Research attachment practices that can help you and your baby bond. And if you find

yourself feeling depressed and uncertain, seek counseling and support. If you want to be weird, stand in front of your bathroom mirror and chant, "I'm going to be a real mom" until you lose your voice. If you want to be normal, buy a baby-carrier to help foster attachment between you and your kiddo.

- **Will I lose myself in motherhood and become "just a mom"?** There will be seasons when you do lose yourself in motherhood. This can be beautifully difficult. Being honest with yourself about your needs is just as important as meeting your child's needs. But will you perhaps find yourself wearing some "mom" jeans and driving a minivan? Yep, anything is possible!

- **What if I don't want to "share" the child with his or her birth parents when it comes to open adoption?** This is something you will have to navigate. My advice is not to make promises you cannot keep. Agree to a level of openness for a season and re-evaluate often. Research open adoption and figure out the pros and cons of every level of openness.

- **What if we're never chosen to adopt?** Most are eventually chosen. Just be you. That's what's most important. You want to be chosen for your wonderful, authentic self.

- **Why did that other couple get chosen and not us?** Comparisons are pointless. There is a right family for every child. A mother has every right to choose the family she sees fit. It wasn't your child; it wasn't your time. Now, go do some online shopping. Buy yourself some non-mom jeans and flaunt them!

Make it Rain

A doption can be really expensive. We all know this. And because of the funds required to bring home your bundle of joy, you may consider fundraising.

Now before we get to fundraising details, let's chat about money.

I see it all the time in adoption groups: people complain about the cost of adoption. And I get it. I know most people don't have a spare twenty or thirty grand laying around. Many who choose to adopt have already spent a chunk of change on fertility treatments or medical bills (as in my case). Despite the stereotypes, most parents who adopt aren't rollin' in the dough.

Most importantly: Choose an adoption professional who is ethical and financially responsible. There is a line between matching expectant (and birth families) with hopeful parents and selling babies. Remember, ethics!

Now here are some things to keep in mind as you financially prepare to adopt:

1: **Utilize the adoption tax credit.** Currently, an over $12,000 credit is available to families who adopt. Keep every single receipt. The IRS is cracking down on fraud.

2: **Employee adoption (reimbursement) assistance.** Some employers offer adoption assistance to their employees, most often paid after the adoption is finalized. Some companies require you to be an employee for a certain time period before you can apply.

3: **Downsize and budget.** Some choose to get older/used cars, move to a different place, get rid of extras like cable television.

4: **Fundraise.** Which leads me to share the "how to."

There a plenty of ways to fundraise: yard sale, silent auction, selling t-shirts, hosting a dinner, open an Etsy shop[41], deliver pizzas (second job!). Some people start a "please help us fund our adoption" page on a crowd-funding site. Julie Gumm, author of *You Can Adopt Without Debt*, outlines some fantastic ideas and tips.

My one prevailing rule about fundraising is this: Don't be tacky.

And because one rule is never enough, here are five sub-rules, ways NOT to be tacky:

1: <u>Don't post your fundraiser every five seconds on all your social media accounts</u>. It makes it seem like you only have friends and followers for your own financial and family-building gain. It's fine to announce that you are raising funds, but don't pester people. Going all-out and constantly reminding friends and family that you need money will only turn them off to your efforts.

2: <u>Don't use the "widows and orphans" Bible verse or the "flesh of my flesh" adoption poem</u>. This verse and poem are overused, and the verse is often taken out of context with the "widow" part omitted. If your faith is part of the reason you are choosing to adopt, just say so. An honest, heartfelt explanation of why you are adopting and what adoption means to you trumps clichés.

3: <u>Don't make financially-irresponsible choices and then expect donations</u>. If you choose to ask for money to help fund your adoption, you will be judged for your lifestyle choices. Asking people to contribute a dollar amount to your fund while your $60,000 SUV is parked in your newly-asphalted driveway doesn't bode well for your ability to manage your money. Your clothing, your home, your extracurricular activities, your vehicles, your dining choices: all will be under a microscope should you choose to ask for financial assistance.

---

41 Anyone else OBSESSED with Etsy?

4: <u>Don't use the savior-and-victim rhetoric</u>. Children are people: people with thoughts, feelings, experiences, and opinions. How you present your adoption fundraising efforts can come back to bite you if you "play up" yourself as a hero or savior and the baby as a charity case. Your words and actions today will matter tomorrow!

5: <u>Don't take it personally when certain people don't contribute</u>. There are so many people and organizations asking for donations, and we all have to pick and choose where we will contribute. Don't assume that just because someone doesn't donate to your fund that they do not support your choice to adopt or that they will not be thrilled when your child comes home. As the leader of a large adoption and fostering support group, I'm invited to a whole lot of fundraising events, and it's not in my budget to contribute to them all.

Whatever route(s) you utilize, just make sure you're making wise choices. My husband (Mr. Finance) would tell you not to take out a second mortgage, borrow against retirement, or rob a bank. (Well, that's a no-brainer, right?) You know the #1 reason couples fight? Money! So don't make dumb decisions that lead you down the road to divorce. You have to think about today *and* tomorrow.

And as far as choosing an adoption professional, please do not go with someone who wants you to put loads of money up front. For one, agencies close. This happened in early 2017 when IAC abruptly closed its doors, leaving hundreds of families brokenhearted and broke. For another, often the money is non-refundable. So if you decide to go with a different agency, choose not to adopt after all, or face an unforeseen life change (job loss, for example), you cannot plead and get your money back.

Be a smart cookie, not a naïve kale smoothie. Got it?

Ultimately, don't be entitled. It's *your* adoption journey and *your* financial responsibility.

Money Really is the Root of All Evil[42]

A ll wine, chocolate, and celebrity Twitter battles aside, we need to have a serious girlfriend chat about ethics. And here's why: *The adoption choices you make today will impact your family, especially your child, forever.*

Money is one of the most important topics in adoption. Where the money is, the power is. As the adopting parent, you have much of the power in the adoption situation. You are likely paying some hefty fees to find and adopt your forever child, and because of this, well, money talks and you get a lot of "say so" in how the adoption goes. Some financial-ethical issues and considerations you may face include:

1: <u>"Birth" parent expenses.</u>

Many agencies and attorneys encourage you to opt into paying what they call "birth parent expenses." This might mean that once you are matched with an expectant mom, you foot her bills. Sometimes this might be something as inexpensive as the occasional gas card, but sometimes it means paying her rent, utility bills, cell phone bill, medical appointment bills, and even buying

---

42 1 Timothy 6:10 had it right!

her maternity clothes and groceries. Paying expenses is quite common these days.

The problem with paying these expenses is that one, it's financially risky. Whether the placement happens or not, the money you pay is non-refundable. Parents often make poor financial choices in order to be able to afford paying these bills, such as borrow against their retirement funds or take out a second mortgage on their homes. By paying just one expectant mom's expenses, you could wipe out your savings, leaving you penniless for another adoption process.

Second, paying mom's expenses isn't something you are doing out of the goodness of your heart. You are doing it because there's a tit-for-tat expectation: expenses paid means you get to adopt the baby. This puts a lot of pressure on a mom to place her baby. What if she decides she really does want to parent? That parenting her baby is the best choice for the baby? Will the mom be able to refuse to place the baby, or will she feel guilty and place out of obligation to the people who paid her expenses?

When deciding to pay expenses or not, and if yes, how much to budget for, check with your adoption professional, honestly analyze what you can afford to risk, know the legal stipulations, and get ethically-oriented.

2: Saying yes or no.

Some agencies charge more for the placement of a white baby and less for the placement of a black or bi-racial baby. (Anyone else find this disturbing?!?) It also leads me to guess that some couples who truly aren't prepared and truly desire to adopt a child of color will be nudged to do so simply because it's either that or not adopt at all. (I have seen agencies charge $40,000 or more for the placement of a white child).

Now, oftentimes parents who adopt children with special needs pay a lesser placement fee; however, in some cases this makes sense given the ongoing expenses a family faces when adopting a child with special needs.

3:    Treatment of expectant mothers.

Unethical agencies push women to place by saying that women who place babies are "selfless" and "heroic," and additionally, give couples who couldn't otherwise have a child the "gift of child." Such agencies might magnify the "perks" of placing a baby while also magnifying the monumental task of choosing to parent in a less-than-ideal situation. Women are presented profiles of families who appear as if they have it all (Disney vacations, Pottery Barn-style homes, and magical holiday celebrations with mountains of gifts under a Martha Stewart Christmas tree) in order to coax them into to lining up the "perfect" family for the child.

Meanwhile, the after-effects of placing a child for adoption may also be minimized: birth mothers are able to "move on" or "get on" with their lives after placement (as if everything goes back to normal). Sometimes moms are offered living expenses paid or even accommodations at a posh maternity home with the expectation that once the baby arrives, the placement will happen. Consider these things when choosing an adoption professional.

4:    Promises that cannot be promised.

Once money enters the picture, mostly because of "birth" parent expenses, some agencies and parents-by-adoption promise mothers openness (as another means of coercion or simple ignorance), but they fail to follow-through. This might mean vowing ongoing communication such as visits with the child, phone calls and Skype sessions, etc.

I don't mean to insinuate that this is done intentionally and maliciously in all cases or even most of cases, because sometimes changes happen. Maybe the child doesn't want ongoing communication when he or she is older. Maybe the family moves far from the birth mother and visits aren't possible. Maybe the agency closes or the social workers turn over, and there is a brokenness or disengagement that occurs between past families and birth parents. And let me say here, open adoption isn't the same as co-parenting, and it certainly isn't a "heal all" for the pain a birth mother goes through at placement for the rest of her life.

5: Expectant mothers are pushed to invest in the needs and desires of the chosen parents.

Again, once money enters the equation, expectant mothers may be prodded by agencies to let their child's intended parents be present in the delivery room or operating room when the baby is born. Another example is agencies pushing mothers to include the prospective parents to attend the mother's medical appointments, participate in birthing classes, and together discuss what the baby's name will be.

Sometimes these things might be what the mother indicates she desires: a growing and close relationship with the parents she's selected. Even if this is what she chooses on her own freewill, there is not guarantee that the mom will place the baby with the chosen couple. Nor is she obligated to do so.

Dishonesty or ignorance from you or from someone who represents you will haunt you, impact you, and result in negative consequences. You cannot brush poor ethics "under the rug" forever. You are responsible for your choices, including your finances and the professional you choose to represent you.

Penny Saver Ads and Rascal Flatts

Piano music begins and scenes of rolling clouds and glorious sunsets and ocean waves crawl across the screen. The screen goes dark for just a moment and then fades, in slow motion, to a close up a couple's faces. They are gazing lovingly at one another, their arms around each other's waists. The camera slowly pans out to show the couple wearing dark-washed jeans, sweaters, and plaid scarfs. The music's volume intensifies. There are sparkly snowflakes falling magically like in a Disney movie. The camera pans out even further to show a message written in the snow: waiting to adopt. The song changes to *God Bless the Broken Road* by Rascal Flatts. Images are layered upon images: the couple on their wedding day, the couple on the beach, the couple surrounded by adorable nieces and nephews, the couple donning aprons and hair nets while serving soup at a homeless shelter. Next, we see photos of their home, including the nursery decorated in a nautical theme. The video ends with an almost complete puzzle on a table, the words "waiting for our missing piece" scrolls across. The music fades, and the video ends with an image of the couple with "please connect with us" and their Twitter, Instagram, and Facebook links.

Cue wiping away tears.

Marketing has changed dramatically in the past several years with the prevalence of social media.

So here's what I want to tell you about this whole self-marketing thing:

- Don't act like a stereotypical used car salesman. (Complete with greasy hair. Girl, wash your hair!)
- Don't assume you will be a better parent than the child's biological parent.
- Don't target women based on their race, clothing, age, job, etc. (If I hear one more hopeful parent talk about handing out their adoption "business" cards to pregnant waitresses and pinning them to bulletin boards at laundry mats on "that" side of town…)[43]
- Don't stand outside an abortion clinic or crisis pregnancy center holding a "waiting to adopt" poster. (Yes, people have done this.)
- Don't assume a woman in a crisis pregnancy should choose adoption ("the loving option").
- Don't place an ad on Craig's List. It's not safe, and frankly, it's just gross.

Stay away the Mark-and-Vanessa Syndrome (you've seen *Juno*, right? I mean, you ARE adopting…).[44] Keep yourself far, far away from the tackiness of the *Penny Saver*.

---

43 Save any and all "pinning" for the ever-addicting and enticing mecca of indulgence: Pinterest.
44 Oh wait, I told you not to watch adoption-themed movies…

No Take Backs

Here are some things you should keep in mind when it comes to sharing your adoption journey, and eventually your child's personal adoption story, online:

1: Do not post photos of someone else, ever, without their permission. Be it Facebook, Twitter, a blog, a message board, or another virtual community. This is especially true of another person's child: even a child in utero (a baby you are matched with who has yet to be born).

2: Do not share expectant or birth family information. This information includes their location, age, situation, physical description, job title, school, etc. It is so easy to track down a person with just the tiniest bit of information about him or her. Adoption is a small, small world.[45]

3: Once information is shared, it cannot be deleted. This is true electronically and mentally. Even if you delete a blog, a Facebook account, or an e-mail, it is still out there in the virtual world, somewhere, and could be found. Once you share information about an adoption situation, someone will always remember that information and can share it, with or without your permission. Remember,

---

45 Disney was right. It's a small world, after all. Now that ridiculous song is stuck in your head, isn't it? You're welcome!

the potential fall-out of oversharing isn't worth the momentary release.

4: Create pseudonyms when sharing adoption information online. What information you do share, create fictional names for the persons involved.

5: When participating in an open adoption, have a conversation about privacy with the other parties involved. Decide what you feel is ok to share via social media and what isn't. Discuss the fact that the young adoptee, despite their age, has a right to privacy of his or her photos and information.

6: Check the laws. As technology advances and the popularity of open adoption increases, the law is gradually catching up. You want to make sure you aren't sharing any information virtually that could lead to a legal issue and that you are respecting the terms of your open adoption.

7: Use your discretion. Be careful who you friend on Facebook, who you follow on Twitter and Instagram, what you share on online message boards, and whom you e-mail. Is your blog private or public? Treat your online interactions as you would your face-to-face interactions: with respect and awareness.

Above all, follow the golden rule: Do unto others as you would have them do unto you. Before you type or click or paste, stop and think: *Will this benefit those who matter most (my child's birth or adoptive parents? My child?) or harm them?*

Are You There God? It's Me, Rachel[46]

We've all heard how powerful, healing, and even stress-relieving prayer can be. And trust me, even if you aren't the praying type (perhaps beyond the time you tried to barter God with an if-You-allow-me-to-win-the-lottery-I-promise-to-donate-half-of-my-winnings-to-something-Jesusy), you will release some form of Judy Blume's famous book title into the sky and hope that God is listening.

Adopting can bring out desperation, hopelessness, confusion, anger, impatience. Thankfully, these hard times also can yield hope, sensitivity, empathy, forgiveness, love, and yes, faith.

When we were waiting to adopt the first time, our profile book was shown to more than ten expectant mothers (ironically, most of whom were going to have Caucasian boys). At first, I went the route of begging God: *Please, please let this mother choose us to parent her child. Please don't let the adoption fail. Please let us get a healthy baby as quickly as possible so that I can stop feeling so sad, so full of yearning, so empty. Steve and I will clearly be awesome parents. We have financial stability. We have love. We have a cute house with a big backyard that will be perfect for a play-set. We have a designated nursery. We are ready. WHERE IS OUR BABY?*

I'm pretty sure God may have rolled His eyes, groaned, and smacked His forehead with His hand at such ridiculously selfish prayer.

---

46 Thank you, Judy Blume and female angst, that sadly, many of us never outgrow.

After a few times of being told "no" and being passed over because another couple was a better fit for the expecting mother or the mom opted to parent, I slowly evolved into a new kind of pray-er. I began to think beyond the unborn (potentially my) baby and my own emotional turmoil, and I considered what the expecting moms might be thinking, feeling, and experiencing.

During our first adoption wait, my husband and I went on vacation. As we were waiting for our next flight at an airport in Chicago, we decided to eat lunch. As we were sitting down to eat, we could hear a young infant crying. The crying got louder and louder, and we turned to see a young woman and a man heading toward a table near us, a baby in her arms.

Soon enough, we struck up a conversation with the young woman and her father, the man she was traveling with. We asked how old her baby was and his name. She smiled like a new mother does and told us that she was a hairdresser, barely making it on her income. She found out she was pregnant and planned to place her baby for adoption. After her son was born, he went into interim care provided by the agency while she took some time to decide if adoption really was what she wanted for her son. After a week of being separated from her child, she decided to parent. With the help of her father, she planned to raise her son.

That was a key moment in our adoption journey, because not only was the young woman once deemed by an agency as a "birth mom" (even though, as we've reviewed, a birth mom is a woman who has terminated her parent rights, not a pregnant woman making an adoption plan or considering adoption) and she shared her story with us (not knowing we were waiting to adopt), but because her son was also bi-racial and we were currently researching and learning about transracial adoption.

In that moment, I realized that behind the terms and roles (such as "birth mom"), there were real women. They weren't mirages, stereotypes, or hypotheticals. They weren't heroes or gift-givers, existing to "bless" poor infertile couples. They weren't brave or selfless women who opted to "give their babies life" (as if all birth and expectant mothers have considered abortion).

My prayers changed from "God, Get me a baby ASAP, please" to "God bless all mothers considering adoption for their babies. Help them make the best choice they can in their individual situations. Please keep watch over the woman who will choose us to be her baby's parents. Give her peace, wisdom, and comfort."

Of course, I had every right to have my own erratic feelings, and I had to continue to work through those (and still do), but when my perception shifted, everything changed. For the better. And forever.

If you haven't yet, seek women who chose to place their kids for adoption. Listen to their stories. Learn. Push past the Miss America mentality: "I wish everyone had a fuzzy kitty and there is world peace" fluff. Dive into the bittersweet, complicated world of adoption: eyes wide open.

For more on navigating the spiritual messiness when adopting and subsequent parenting, check out the book I co-authored with Madeleine Melcher (2015): *Encouragement for the Adoption and Parenting Journey: 52 Devotions and a Journal.*

Let's Make Like Kindergarten: The Letter of the Day Is

t's my book, so my rules. But I promise, these will help you as you consider adopting, wait to adopt, accept the placement of your baby, and parent. Here's the deal. Everything you need to know boils down to words all starting with a single letter: E. Here you go:

1: <u>Make decisions out of education, not ignorance.</u>

I know the word "ignorance" is a big turn off, but let me tell you what ignorance means. It means: fear, confusion, apathy, avoidance. Ignorance is not bliss. While you're waiting to adopt and even after you have adopted, you need to relentlessly pursue education. This means reading books (hey, look at you! You're already accomplishing something in this department!) and articles, joining an adoption support group, talking to triad members about their experiences, attending conferences and classes. It means you are "doing" (and not "did"). Education should never end. Because when you are educated, you can make better choices along the journey. You're more authentically confident.

2: <u>Empathy wins.</u>

Of course, we know "love wins" (thank you, Glennon Melton Doyle): but if you've been in the adoption community for any longer than five seconds, you know that love isn't enough. Love is absolutely the foundation, the motivator, but it is meant to be built upon! In any situation, adoption and subsequent parenting, empathy is critically important. When your child struggles with being an adoptee, empathy wins. When your child's birth mother cancels a visit, empathy wins. When your child struggles with the idea of a new sibling, empathy wins. When your partner is in a valley, struggling with surrendering the plan to have a biological child, empathy wins. Empathy doesn't make you a doormat. Empathy is a springboard to better tomorrows. (Wow, do I sound like a greeting card or what?)

3: <u>Ethics should be at the forefront.</u>

I tell my children all the time: make good choices. Good choices (usually) result in good things. And bad choices? They always come back to haunt you.

When are educated and empathetic, you naturally desire to be ethical. With every choice you make, you ask yourself, what is the ethical decision?

I've talked about ethics throughout the book, so you're probably like, "Really, Rachel? AGAIN?" Yes, sister. Again. Because ethics are that important! And at this point, you're this far into the book, and you have wrapped your head around what ethics are, how to make ethical choices, and especially, especially, why it's so damn important! Because every choice you make has a forever-impact, especially on your child.

4: <u>Surround yourself (and your family) with encouragement.</u>

Being a mama-by-adoption presents unique challenges, challenges not discussed in typical mommy groups where the conversations tend to turn to breastfeeding and pregnancy cravings. You need a village of your own that meets your needs (adoption triad members, families of color if you adopt transracially, families parenting children with special needs if you adopted a child with needs, etc.). You need experienced people who get you and who will, above all, offer you encouragement so you can keep doing what you were chosen to do: parent your child.

Additionally, your child needs encouragement. Being around other children who are like them (in race, ability, or adoption "status") is imperative. These relationships foster community: belonging. We all want to belong!

Yes, committing to finding and investing time and energy into your village means putting yourself "out there." It requires vulnerability and courage. It requires a deep sense of humility. This is what your child needs from you. Take the steps. Do the work. You've got this!

5: Empowerment.

Empowerment: confidence, determination, relentless commitment, strength. This is what you will gain by following the other Es I've shared with you here. I'm not talkin' about a power-trip, a big ego, or snobbery. I'm talking about reaching the peak of what you've worked so hard for so that you can be the parent your child needs you to be.

When you are empowered you don't hesitate to ask for help. And you sure don't hesitate to help others. You don't spend weeks thinking about ethics, because you KNOW what the right choice is (even when it's difficult, you're still gonna do the right thing!). You don't bury your head in the sand (even if it's ice-white and you have a tropical drink in your hand), you don't sugar-coat, and you don't apologize for having both joy and sadness (sounds like an animated movie, right?). You are always learning and loving.

Alright! Good job, class! You learned all about the letter E. Milk and cookies time!

What's in a Name? Uh, a lot

n case you haven't noticed, naming your child is a huge freaking deal these days. I mean, just look at celebrities trying up one another with the most outrageous names for their precious children. (Ahem: North and Apple).

For the love of all things chocolate, please do not name your child Rainbow Priscilla-Anastasia Buttercup. I was at Target (naturally: where else would I be?) when I heard a mom call out to her toddler: "Come back here, Clementine!" It took her way too long to yell at her child, because Clementine just doesn't flow well from the mouth. I had to stifle my urge to respond, "Oh my darlin', oh my darlin', oh my darlin', Clementine!" in a twangy voice. I also began thinking of all the other fruits a child could be named that are equally as ridiculous, including, kumquat, pineapple, banana, and starfruit.[47]

Here are my rules for naming a child:

1: <u>The name must pass the resume test.</u> Sadly, employers might choose (purposefully or unintentionally) to discriminate based on an applicant's name. I wish this weren't the case, but it is. Thus...

2: <u>Unique names are fine (as long as they meet guidelines 1, 5, and 6), but I'm not naming my kid an exotic flower, my favorite weather</u>

---

47 I am a writer. My imagination runs wild. And I do love fruit.

element, or hummus. Listen, I love kiwi, but I'm not naming my child after it.

4: If I can't yell it easily, I'm not choosing it. And trust me, you may have every intention of being a "peaceful" and "gentle" parent who walks around as if you came out of the womb doing yoga and sipping coconut water, but there will come a day when you yell. The sooner you accept this, the happier you will be.

5: The initials must not spell an inappropriate word. This should be a given. Monograms spelling out: SUK, or ASS, or DAM, or COC: not happening.

6: The child doesn't get two or three middle names. I have two middle names. It's been a pain on paperwork my entire life. Pick and stick.

7: We don't choose a name on the most popular 100 list. Again, this is our personal preference.

In complete seriousness, it's always a good idea to consider what the child's birth family wants. Will you co-name the baby? Will you list some favorite names and the birth family will choose the name? Will the birth family name the child? Should you incorporate your child's racial culture into his or her name? None of these are best or right, but they are things you should consider.

In the case of our adoptions, we elected to combine our children's birth names with the names we had chosen. We felt that it was very special for our children to have the gift of a name from birth family along with knowing that the name we chose for the child was something meaningful to us.

If you elect to name your kid Hershey Tanktop Obadiah Guacamole, he will definitely get some attention, and not in a good way. Don't ask me for sympathy. I warned you.

What's in a Name: Round 2

S o you still have burning questions regarding names, don't you? Let's get to those questions!

Q: Is it ok to name my son after my husband, you know, making our son a "junior"?
A: It is your child, right? So, yes.

Q: Should I be expected to co-name the baby with the baby's birth parents?
A: Whatever you do, just be honest. If you have no intention of co-naming the baby, don't say you will. If you're open to co-naming, say so.

Q: Everyone wants to know what names we like. Do I share or keep those names a secret?
A: Personally, I prefer to keep names we like to ourselves. First, I don't want the feedback from others (particularly any snarly facial expressions). Second, it's our decision, one that may not manifest as intended if we do co-name the child with the birth parents. But hey, do what you want. Just prepared that not everyone will think the unique name of Dandelion Moscato is cute.

Q: We'd love to give our kiddo a family name. Is that ok, considering the child's start wasn't with our family?

A: Of course! Your child, once adopted, is your child! However, you can consider honoring both the child's birth family and your family by choosing a first and middle name that honors both families.

Q: Is it wrong to change my child's birth name?

A: When a mom has a baby, she has the right to put whatever name she chooses on the birth certificate. This name can be changed by the parents who adopt the baby. Is it ok to do so? Well, what did you and the child's birth parents agree to? Whatever you say, you need to do. Also consider that some adult adoptees like that their parents gave them a special name (such as a family name, a name the parents liked, etc.), while others wish they would have retained their birth name. There is no way to know what your child will desire in the future, so you have to use your best judgement now: you know, parenting the best you can like parents do!

Q: We had a name picked out that we loved, and then we experienced a failed adoption. Should we use that name for our future child, or is it a bad idea?

A: I think it really depends on your grief process. Is using the name again for the child who will be yours going to cause you sadness and remorse, or will it bring about healing and happiness? Go with your gut on this one.

In Case You Kick the Bucket

Many young and middle age adults don't have guardianship established for their children in the case that something happens to the parents. This is foolish and irresponsible, especially in a case where the children were adopted. And here's why.

If you have an open adoption, if your child was adopted transracially, if your child has special needs, these are all circumstances where choosing your child's guardians need to be taken into consideration. The person or people you choose to step in should something happen to you need to be qualified and agreeable to what is best for your child.

As you think through whom you will establish as your child's guardian, I suggest making a list of what is important to you parenting wise, but also what is important for your particular child. This list should consist of: a list of musts (this person must be able/willing to do these things for my child), a list of wishes (this would be ideal, but it's not a requirement), and a list of deal-breakers. This will help you make the best decision for your child.

Once you decide who you wish to name as your child's guardian, ask the person, and please detail why you have selected him or her. Make clear what's important to you and why, giving the person a fair chance to decide if he or she feels okay with the situation. I recommend a face to face conversation, not a text with a coffin or skull emoji. Don't make it weird(er).

Though none of us like to think about something tragic forcing us to separate us from our child, establishing a guardian is a way of ensuring our child's well-being should something happen.

Boo Boos

So one thing your social worker may tell you to do is start looking for a doctor for your future child. This sounds totally easy-peasy, right? Just ask your mom friends which doctor they recommend, and then that's the doctor you choose.

As a person with a chronic disease, I can't express enough how important it is that you choose a great doctor for your little bundle of joy. While you're waiting to adopt, schedule a consult with each doctor you are considering. This should be free of charge. Here are some considerations:

1: Does this doctor have experience with adoptees and adoption? Many kiddos who were adopted do not have a complete or reliable medical history. Some do not have any medical history at all. Furthermore, doctors with little to no experience with adoptees might use inappropriate adoption language and ask questions just to be nosy instead of sticking to medically necessary conversations. Be sure to ask: "How much experience do you have with adoptees and adoption?" versus "Do you have experience with adoptees and adoption?" (which generates a simple yes or no response). Just because the doctor doesn't have much experience, doesn't mean he or she isn't a good medical professional. If the person is willing to be educated, the doctor may still be an ok fit for you and your child.

2: Does this doctor have experience with the possible situations your child could face such as drug exposure/withdrawals, RAD (Reactive

Attachment Disorder), trauma, sensory issues (which adoptees are at more of a risk of experiencing), premature birth and the effects of that, etc.? Remember, ask open-ended questions, not questions eliciting a simple yes or no response. For example, "What do you know about RAD?" vs. "Do you have a good understanding of RAD?"

3: Does the doctor have good bedside manner with children? A patient and doctor relationship is so important when it comes to a child's health and well-being. If you don't get a great vibe from the doctor, it's OK to continue your search. (I once interviewed a pediatrician who didn't even introduce herself to my kids and didn't use a "kid voice" when speaking to them. Another pediatrician we interviewed asked my daughters to introduce themselves, and when they did she responded, while gesturing toward my toddler son, "I couldn't hear you girls because of Mr. Noisy over here." As you can guess, she's not our pediatrician.)

4: Does the doctor make you feel welcome and comfortable? Babies have a lot of medical appointments in the first year, and they have even more if they have any health issues. You need to feel at ease speaking to this doctor. (Judging the doctor's wardrobe is totally and completely reasonable, as well. I'm joking. Sort of.)

5: Does the doctor offer Saturday hours, equally-as-qualified physician assistants and nurses, an after-hours phone number, etc.? These are questions all parents-to-be should ask. If they are only open every other Tuesday from 12:46-3:14, it's probably not the ideal office. Children will always get sick two minutes before a doctor's office closes for a three day weekend. So with that in mind, make sure you know where the nearest Urgent Care facility is located.

6: How is the front desk staff? The front desk is the "gateway" to communication with the doctor, with billing, and with medical questions. If the staff is slow to answer the phone, return your calls, or isn't pleasant and polite, that's a deal breaker, even if the doctor is fantastic. If you are met with blank stares, offered a Dum Dum sucker (instead of a mini wine bottle) or a sticker (generic, not licensed Disney), or grunts (Are you pooping?), proceed to the nearest exit, pronto.

7: <u>Does the doctor recommend that new moms drink lattes and eat scones until 5:00 p.m. and then switch to wine and brownies for a well-balanced mommy diet?</u> If not, find a new doctor. I mean really, can just anyone be a doctor these days?

All Aboard the Cliché Train

There are many adoption phrases you will become very familiar with. They're all over t-shirts, decorative signs, and even some adoption agency websites and blogs. Here's what they are, and why they suck.

Now before you label me as the ultimate adoption Debbie Downer, I want you to know something: words matter. How you talk about adoption, and ultimately about your child and his or her story, has consequences (positive or negative). I tend to err on the side of caution and also know that many experienced triad members have strong feelings about adoption clichés. It's important that we listen to experienced voices, consider, and honor.

"I carried my child in my heart, not in my womb."

This is the cheesiest of adoption sayings. First, it minimizes the significance and magnitude of the birth mother's pregnancy and connection to the child. Second, there is no correlation between the birth mother carrying her child and the adoptive mother "carrying" the child in her heart. I much prefer the adoption triangle (a triangle with a heart in it) signifying the union of three persons: adoptee(s), adoptive parent(s), and birth parent(s). The sides are equal and together they create a beautiful shape that interconnects them.

"DNA doesn't make a family; love makes a family."

Technically, biology (DNA) did create the first family. And no matter what happens, whether the adoption is completely open and healthy and happy, or the adoption is closed with lots of mystery and uncertainty, the adoption wouldn't happen without the first family. Though DNA isn't a ticket to being a forever family, biology does matter. I have seen this so clearly in my own children, all of whom have open adoptions with their birth families. The resemblance to their birth families is incredibly clear. Not only do they physically resemble their birth families, but their personalities, their talents, their gestures, many of these come from their first families. There is simply no reason to put a hierarchy in place, ranking the birth family and the adoptive family. Nature and nurture play a part in the child's life, and DNA does create a family. This saying sounds like a "take that" to biological families, so it's not something I'll be using.

"Adopted children are gifts."

To me, a gift is a thing, an object. A child is a person, a human, with thoughts, feelings, opinions, and personalities. They are not at all the same. Giving a gift reminds me of Christmas, or a birthday, but certainly not the passing of a child between a biological parent and adoptive parent. Adoption is complicated, so it can hardly be packaged as a pretty statement referencing gift-giving and gift-receiving. The objectification of a child is bothersome. Yes, my children are incredible, and I'm very thankful to be their mother, but they aren't presents.

"Adoption is the new pregnant."

Adoption and pregnancy are not the same in any way, shape, or form. Furthermore, adoption isn't a bandwagon to be joined. Choosing to adopt or place a child for adoption should be carefully considered, not made haphazardly, because ultimately, the adoption has a tremendous impact on the trajectory of the child's life. To me, adoption is a serious, life-altering decision, whether it's placing or becoming an adoptive parent. The adoption process and action cannot be summarized or referenced into this light-hearted, attempt-at-humor comment.

"Adopted kids are so lucky!"

This is often said as a result of what the media has taught the public about adoption. It is assumed that all adoptees came from abusive or neglectful circumstances, their biological parents fit a certain bill (young, drug abusers, sexually promiscuous, irresponsible, poor), and that the adoptive parents are the saviors who gave the adoptee "a good home." Furthermore, adoptees shouldn't be made to feel that they should feel grateful for being adopted or that they were rescued by their adoptive parents. Adoptive parents are quite ordinary, and many, when asked, chose adoption because they wanted to grow their family. It's not necessary for them to be put on a pedestal.

"Never underestimate the power of an adoptive mom."

Though adoptive parenting can be different in some ways, an "adoptive mother" is first and foremost a mother. A real mother. Any person put on a pedestal is bound to disappoint those who put her on it in the first place. Furthermore, having higher expectations of a mother who adopted her children puts a lot of pressure on the mom to make sure her children are perfect. This is simply not fair to the mother or the child. The family was formed in a way that isn't common, but this doesn't mean the family is overwhelmingly different, special, or deserving of applause or criticism.

"Keep calm and adopt on!"

This saying is ridiculous for a few reasons. First, keeping calm during an adoption process? Who is laughing with me? Second, adoption is simply not simple. To summarize and glorify it like "Rock on!" is not anywhere close to the true nature of adoption. I know the "keep calm" sayings are quite popular right now, used for everything from baking to studying to parenting, but applying anything along the lines of "calm" and "keep on" to those of us in the trenches of adoption just isn't going to fly.

Meeting the Stranger Carrying Your Possible-Maybe-Future Baby

The social worker calls: an expectant mother wants to meet you. You're over-the-moon! You hang up the phone and immediately call your partner (or your best friend, or your grandma) and exclaim the exciting news.

Then it hits you: you are meeting an expectant mother. The woman who might be carrying your possibly-maybe future baby. Gulp.

First, let me tell you, she's nervous too. I know you're a wreck. You are analyzing everything from what shade of lipstick to wear to the brand of your partner's socks. (Yep, you're that ridiculous right now.) Maybe you should whiten your teeth? Highlight your hair? Nail polish or no nail polish? You ask your neighbor, "Is my laugh weird?" You are freaking out.

But the woman you are about to meet is carrying a baby and is considering placing him or her into your arms forever. That's a big, big, big deal. Way bigger of a deal than your hair color.

Second, I get it. You've spent the past few months being judged. Or so you feel. I guess a better word might be scrutinized, analyzed, or assessed. The homestudy process is intrusive. And now you're up for a big interview. No wonder you're feeling overwhelmed and fearful and anxiety-ridden!

Third, and the most importantly, I need you do to this: just be yourself. Be yourself. Remember when we talked about that when you were creating your profile book? You want to be chosen for exactly who you are: weird laugh and all. If you aren't the right fit for this expectant mom and her baby, so be it. Show up and be you.

An FAQ: *What should I take with me?*

If it's a first meeting, I suggest a few family photo albums to show. If you've already been chosen by this mother, buy a small photo album and fill it with pics from around your town, places the child will go: the local school, the donut shop, the library, the park, etc. Keep in mind that this will clearly show your location; therefore, if you're adoption isn't one with a lot of openness, this may not be the best idea. You can also take a small gift (if laws and rules allow) such as flowers, a blank journal, or a small pampering gift basket. Do not take anything expensive or assuming. Take something you'd give any expecting mother. If you're a crafty person, take something you've made.

Then just show up. Not in wedding attire, please. Just dress nicely and comfortably, and go.

A good agency worker will facilitate the conversation. Don't assume the mom is going to place and interrogate her with questions. Stay in your lane. Ask how she's feeling, ask about her likes and dislikes, ask what she wants to know about you. If there's a lull in the conversation, bring out your family photo albums. Don't ask about her hospital plan, if you can name the baby, or if she wants to come over for the baby's first birthday party. Chill out. This isn't a sprint.

Meetings can be nerve-racking. They can also be very telling. Maybe you get a vibe that the match isn't right for you. That's OK. Or maybe you connect well with the expectant mother. Just let whatever happens happen.

I know, so vague right? I'm sorry I cannot offer you more assurance or comfort. I know exactly how sitting in a meeting feels, having met three birth parents months prior to placement. The meetings were this strange cocktail of awkward, emotional, tense, encouraging, and uncertain. It's like nothing I've ever experienced. But I showed up, was myself, and then waited. Because that's what we parents-by-adoption do: we wait, and wait, and wait.

After the meeting, you'll be a bit sweaty, emotionally tired, and hungry. You'll want all the carbs. This is normal.

In conclusion (because the English teacher in me thinks it's so funny when students wrote "in conclusion" in their essays because duh, of course it's the conclusion since it's the last paragraph), adoption is weird. The sooner you accept this, the better off you'll be. Now go get some salty carbs.

Token of Appreciation

Let's talk about gifting, because it's a major topic in the adoption community.

When you are meeting with an expectant mother who is thinking about choosing adoption, when an expectant mother chooses you to be the parents of her baby, when you're visiting an expectant mother in the hospital after she's just given birth to the baby you are matched with: these are all opportunities to give gifts. But should you?

I'm a believer in the Love Languages coined by Dr. Gary Chapman.[48] My top Love Language is gifts. And I once heard Dr. Chapman say, we often love others using our primary love language, meaning, the way we like to be loved is how we love others.

I share this to humbly admit to you that I find immense joy and connection by finding the perfect gift for someone. It's even better if it's a collection of small gifts. I'm the girl who still sends family members birthday cards via snail mail. I take a struggling friend a bottle of wine and a good book. And I buy my kids little gifts for every minor holiday, usually books, because I just cannot help myself. So believe me when I say that when we were adopting (four times), I really had to reign in my gift-giving tendencies.

You might be wondering why. What's the big deal? I know you want to impress an expectant mother. I know you want to show up with something

---

48 *The Five Love Languages: The Secret to Love That Lasts*, by Dr. Gary Chapman (2015)

that says "thank you" and "I care." And for some of us (like me), showing up anywhere empty-handed goes against who we are.

You probably already know what I'm going to say: ethics. Anything that's "tit for tat" in adoption, no matter how well-intended, can complicate things. Now I know, a bouquet of flowers at the hospital doesn't exactly say, "Thanks for your baby." But all the little things (gifts, texts, visits) can add up to undue stress on the expectant mother (and father), perhaps making her feel guilty if she is considering parenting.

I did not refrain from gifts completely in our adoptions: before placement or after. However, I was very mindful of what I was giving and when, and I always carefully evaluated the WHY. Ethics starts with your heart and your motivations. How you manifest your ethical foundation is important.

Don't give a gift to show off. Don't give a gift to convince. Don't give a gift to coerce. Don't give a gift to prove.

A good guideline is this: do what you would do for any other special person in your life. If your cousin had a baby, what would you bring her? If your dad was celebrating his birthday, what would he appreciate? This isn't to say gift-giving is one-size-fits all. It's not. But as far as monetary value, stay within your norm, your means, and above all, your ethics.

Ding, Dong, Ditch: When Adopting Feels Like a Prank

You might have many or few profile showings during your wait for your child, but no matter what, each possibility will have you elated and deflated if you aren't chosen. You will question everything from the shape of your big toe to the existence of God. Let me tell you, this is completely normal, though when you're in the midst of another "no," you feel anything but normal.

We had over ten profile showings during our first adoption wait. At one point, I was just so hopeful we'd finally be chosen that I crept to Kohl's and let myself buy a baby girl outfit. Somehow I had determined that if I actually whipped out my credit card and brought that outfit home, we'd most certainly become parents to the little girl. But let me tell you, going from rack to rack under the florescent lights, I felt like a fraud. I wasn't a mommy, so how dare I go shopping like one?

We weren't chosen, again, and the tiny pink outfit got returned.

Listen, sister. Adopting and adoption often make no sense at all. You will absolutely feel as if you boarded a never-ending roller coaster. There will be moments of elation when your soul is flooded with hope and you are twirling in an imaginary field of butterflies, a vibrant rainbow in the sky. Then the next minute, you're curled up on your couch surrounded by crumpled tissues, and you are certain that no one will ever choose your pathetic, mascara-streaked, drippy-nosed self to parent a baby.

The number one question many have when adopting is how long will they wait for a baby. Will it takes just weeks? Months? Years? The wait is absolute torture. Minutes feel like days. Control and faith are juxtaposed. Hope and fear are constantly colliding. It's like you're a Midwesterner thrust into the heart of a hurricane. You have no idea what to do.

I want you to go back to the chapter I called "Ready, Set, Wait," and I want you to make a list. Because you need to do something more productive than watch those asinine Lifetime movies I warned you about! This list needs to have at least three points, three reminders, of what you should be doing right now to prepare for future motherhood. It might be reading an adoption book, joining a yoga class, and planning a mini-vaca with your partner. Take your list, stick it somewhere visible, and then make it your mission to do those things.

And for the love of pacifiers, join an adoption support group.

Squirrel!

ne of our favorite animated movies is *Up*, especially because we adore the little wilderness explorer name Russell, the old guy who is grumpy (turned loving), and the dog. Because that dog is SO easily distracted. He's just chillin' when a squirrel skirts by, and then the dog is ON. Sometimes when I'm talking to my husband and he randomly brings up whatever he's thinking about, I interrupt him and say, "Squirrel!"

Alright, so here's a break so we can chat about random adoption questions that don't really have a place in another chapter. Disorganized? Yeah, a bit. Necessary? Of course! I'm not here to waste your time. Here we go with what I'm calling the squirrel questions:

The expectant mom refuses to name the birth father, which makes me nervous. What should we do?

It's the mom's right not to name the father, but I'm leery of this because the birth father has rights, too. He did help create the baby. As to why a mom won't name the baby's father, well there can be a myriad of reasons. Some might be legit (he's a rapist or an abuser) and some might be "other" (she doesn't know who the father is, she doesn't want the father to stop the adoption, her family might be upset with her if they knew the father's identity, etc.). If you proceed with this adoption, you need to do so with eyes wide open. An adoption attorney can help you navigate the birth father's rights and the legalities of notification and termination. There is no right or wrong answer here, but of course, you should always err on the side of ethics.

I just can't get excited about this match because I feel like at any moment, everything will fall apart. The social worker will call and say mom is parenting. How can I get out of this funk?
Oh, sister, I've been there. Waiting to see what will happen is about as fun for me as when I rode Expedition Everest at Disney World. (Me: clawing husband's arm, eyes tightly shut, and repeating over and over, "This isn't real, this isn't real, this isn't real." Then when the ride was over I found the nearest fake-rock, fell upon it, and swore I'd NEVER ride that thing again.) There is simply no way around the pain, doubt, fear, and anxiety. You've got to walk through it. This is the adoption journey. However, there are some things you can avoid: like refreshing your e-mail every four seconds, trying to dig up info on the expectant parents on social media, and eating so much ice cream. Get out. Go for a walk, have coffee with a friend, go to dinner with your husband, learn a new craft. These things won't eliminate the struggle, but they will help.

My parents keep talking about our future "adopted child." I'm so happy they're excited to welcome a grandbaby, but I can't stand the referral to our child as "adopted." What do I say to them?
Yay for grandparents! But it sounds like they need some adoption education. I highly recommend getting them two books: *Adoption is a Family Affair: What Relatives and Friends Must Know* and *In On It: What Adoptive Parents Would Like You To Know About Adoption. A Guide for Relatives and Friends*. Let them learn at their own pace, just as you have. As for the issue presently at hand, the next time the g-parents-to-be refer to their future grandchild as your "adopted child," just say, "I love how excited you are! But if you refer to the child as 'adopted' all the time, it can be othering. Of course, adoption will be an open, honest, and ongoing conversation, but the child will just be our child, not our 'adopted' child." Chances are, they are just really excited and, as all of us are at the beginning of our adoption journeys, ignorant to the appropriate language. They probably don't realize the implications of their phrasing, so pointing it out to them now will avoid hurt feelings and awkwardness later.

I'm jealous. My co-workers have baby showers for any pregnant lady in our group, but when I announced I was adopting, there was no shower. It's hard to attend all the celebrations while being excluded from the expecting-mommy goodness. Do I say something or suffer in silence?

I understand your pain! It can be difficult to be the woman coming into motherhood in a non-traditional way. I honestly think that many people don't know how to react or what to do in certain situations, adoption being one of them, so they just don't do anything versus risking offending you by doing the wrong thing. Directly demanding a shower in your honor is rude, but it's perfectly fine to discuss your feelings with the party planner. I don't mean desperately asking for a shower while sobbing on her shoulder until you soak her blouse with your salty tears, but I think some transparency about waiting for a baby with no due date has been hard for you and attending the showers for pregnant mommies can bum you out. If that results in a shower in your honor, great. And if not, you'll have to decide whether or not to attend the showers of your co-workers or skip the festivities. Not out of spite, but because you're not in a good emotional place to genuinely contribute to the happiness of another person.

I'm reading everything about adoption that I can get my hands on, researching nursery furniture, and browsing baby name websites. But my partner seems much less interested in the baby prep. Does this mean he doesn't want to adopt? How do I get him on board the Excitement Train?

First, is this a personality difference? Are you usually the planner and executor? Are you more type A and your partner is more chill? Second, could it be that you're nesting (yep, moms who adopt nest too) and your partner isn't? No need to jump to worst case scenarios. Third and most importantly, ask your partner how he's feeling about the adoption journey and pending parenthood. It could be that you're preparing yourselves in different ways. He might be respecting your need to nest. But if you're feeling lonely, say so. And it might be time to take a (small) step back from focusing so much on the adoption process and make sure you're nurturing yourselves as a couple. Because once the baby comes, it'll be ALL about the child and you'll have far less time to sleep in, go to dinner, and have uninterrupted conversations and times of intimacy. There is no right way to wait for a baby, and it's OK to process what's going on in different ways.

The mom we're matched with insists on naming the baby and expects we keep that name. To be honest, I hate the name she's chosen. It doesn't at all fit our preferences or flow with our last name. So, what do we do?
Wow. How awkward, right? Well, you know what I'm going to tell you: ethics. Which means, you need to be honest. If you don't intend to keep the name the mom chooses, you must tell her that. I know what you're thinking: if we speak up, she may choose a different family. And you would be justified in thinking that. But it's never OK to be dishonest. I suggest speaking to your adoption worker about your feelings and getting guidance on how to best approach the expectant mom: but you MUST speak honestly. You can suggest a compromise, such as co-naming the baby and explain why.

Quit Surfing

One of the worst things a hopeful or new parent-by-adoption can do is surf the Internet. If you've been considering adoption for any increment of time, you know what I mean.

Online groups have their place, but only if you have a thick skin and believe that what is healthy is anything in moderation (except drugs, crime, and meatloaf; I hate meatloaf). It is helpful to be able to read, with the tap of a finger, the experiences of hundreds, even thousands, of people from all over the world.

But what you get online is usually one of two extremes: the ones who are so, so, so over-the-moon happy about adoption that they spend their days telling everyone how magical and beautiful it is or the ones who experienced traumatizing events that leave them bitter and very angry (justifiably so).

So you decided to ask a question. It could be something as completely innocent as, "What is the best children's adoption book?" and you'll have virtual rotten tomatoes thrown at you. You will be pounced on by both camps, and usually, it's not even about you. Online group politics are no joke. They're just throwing their virtual rotten tomatoes at each other, but you're stuck in the middle and are bound to get hit.

Congratulations. You are now more frustrated, confused, and disheartened as ever.

So what do you do? The next day, you go surfing again.

It's not a good cycle. It leads to carb loading (without the intention of running a marathon) and thus, weight gain. Great. It also leads to self-doubt, more fear, and even tears, because your adoption-weary soul cannot deal.

You know the saying, right? Shame on them if they fool you once, but shame on you if they fool you twice.

Listening to experienced members of the adoption triad (remember, that's parents who have adopted, birth parents, and adoptees) has many benefits. I mean, I write and speak about adoption for a living, after all! But relying solely on strangers on the Internet to affirm you, educate you, or guide you is foolish.

Stop hiding behind your screen. Go out and make some real friends in the adoption community. People you can put your arms around. People you can sit across the table from while you sip coffee. People you can invite into your home. People you can see eye-to-eye with, literally and figuratively. People who are just a phone call, a text, or a short drive away. People who have your back when the poo hits the fan. People who offer give-and-take. People who can hold your hand, your actual hand. People who can gently correct you when you are wrong. People who can steer you in the right direction. People who can give you an encouraging smile and word.

You know what you need? An adoption support group. I've only mentioned that about a dozen times so far in this book. You need to be in an adoption support group. No excuses.

Make sure your village consists of all triad members, not just fellow parents-by-adoption. You need the wisdom of adoptees and birth parents. Hearing their stories, even when they are difficult, will benefit you as parent raising an adoptee. You need to be in a place where you feel both safe and challenged, empowered and educated. If they serve tacos at meetings, you know you've found the right place!

I know some of you are introverts. You have anxiety. You think your insecurities are tattooed on your forehead. You are fearful of judgement. Frankly, you are fearful of fear. And I get it. Choosing to adopt is big and scary and hard. It's loud. It can be overwhelming and overpowering. It's easier to sit behind a screen and lurk. But honestly, it doesn't get the job done.

If you are going to be the parent your child needs, please put yourself out there. Yes, you may mess up sometimes, but that's called being human. Yes, you may not be friended by the first person you approach. Not everyone is meant to be your friend. Yes, you may have to open up to people you barely know in an attempt to establish a friendship. But the risk is worth the reward.

Every parent-by-adoption has a beginning mark. And the ones who stay at the mark, lingering, never progress and never blossom into the guide their child needs. It's safer to stay-put in the moment, but it's very dangerous for the long-term wellbeing of the family.

Stop surfing today. Spend your time and energy engaging in real community, real friendship, and real growth.

I Fell in Love with a Child Who Wasn't Mine: A Love Letter to Our Fourth Baby[49]

I fell in love with a child who wasn't mine.

I told myself not to.

I tried to set up walls, boundaries, and guards.

But I failed.

I failed desperately, miserably, and soon enough, willingly.

I imagined what it would be like to hang up SIX stockings on the mantle instead of the usual five.

I thought about our future trip to Disney World, when we'd board the plane, and we'd get to take up TWO FULL rows of seats instead of three on one side, and two on the other, leaving a poor stranger to awkwardly sit next to me and one of my kids.

I created a note on my phone and listed all the baby names I loved. I spent HOURS on that list.

Then I slowly began buying things for the baby we were matched with. And soon, she had an all out nursery. A nursery without a baby. Hopefully awkward. Hopelessly surrendered.

I researched newborn photographers and pediatricians.

I prayed. I prayed for peace. For certainty. For others. For myself.

---

49 This has been one of my most popular blog posts, so I had to include it in the book. Enjoy!

I counted down. Date after date, milestone after milestone (in the journey that seemingly was never ending). This helped me believe I had order, control, and organization.

We chose a name from the list off my phone. But I couldn't say her name aloud. Because then she was "her" and "the baby."

We walked around with a little secret growing in our hearts. And sometimes we let the secret slip out. We were expecting. Maybe. Sort-of. We shall see.

I knew the risks. The possibilities. The heart-makes and heartaches. I knew my fantasy could crumble at any minute.

I stood grounded in ethics which collided a thousand times a day with my heart-pulls. I learned they could co-exist, but it was uncomfortable. And scary. Very scary.

I loved and loved and loved bigger and bigger, knowing that there was a risk (the elephant in the room) of shattering, disappearing, and losing.

I knew that the nursery I had lovingly put together could remain empty forever. I bought little shoes and diapers and picture frames to fill. Yet I kept every single receipt. That little pile of papers, clipped together neatly, tortured me.

I listened to God tell me, one day when I was finishing up a workout, "Stop waiting for something to bad to happen." Then I told God that wasn't possible. Then I questioned if it was my own helpless illusions that spoke to me or if it really were God bestowing some fatherly-ness upon my anxiety-ridden soul.

I nested. I organized a closet here. I straightened up the books there. I purged and sorted and tidied. I needed something to do with my energy and neurotic tendencies.

I remember now, on the other side of the Wait (capital W to symbolize a very stressful era in my life), one of my favorite quotes. I find comfort in it. That despite the risks, I loved big and loved well. I loved a birth family (who was not yet a "birth" family) and a baby (not yet "my" baby).

"'Tis better to have loved and lost than never to have loved at all," wrote Alfred Lord Tennyson.[50]

---

50 From his poem "In Memoriam A.H.H." (1849)

It took courage, it took steadfastness and commitment, it took unclench-ing, and it took faith. Immense faith. It took uttering "it is well with my soul" a thousand times a day, an hour.

I am guilty of doing the thing I said I would never do: I fell in love with a child who wasn't mine.

But now she is mine. And I'm grateful that I can tell her, "I loved you before I knew you, before I held you, before I heard you. I loved you big: even though it was hard. Even though it was scary. I fell in love with you, I prayed for you. I loved you in the ways I could, in the place I was in, and I am thankful that I took the risk: the risk of loving at the risk of losing, because it was better than not loving at all."

When You're in a Funk: And I'm Not Talkin' About Uptown Funk

No matter where you are in your journey: considering adoption, working on all that homestudy paperwork (aka: tree murdering), waiting (and waiting and waiting and waiting) for your first child, post-placement (and facing some obstacles), or in-route to adopting again, it will happen. You will find yourself in a funk, also known as Adoption Burnout.

Your funk may just be a weeks-on-end bad mood. It might be the big ol' green-eyed monster (AKA jealousy) ripping your heart to shreds. It might be the third cutesy "sprinkle" or baby shower invite that landed in your inbox with a perky ding. It could be the adoption "advice" (also known as Judgement 101) you received from a family member or friend. It could be that "due date" you were asked to put on the online baby registry you play around with at 1 a.m. Whatever is going on in your journey, being in a funk is nothing short of miserable.

Now, I'm sorry to tell you that there's no quick and easy way to get out of a funk. I know, I'm supposed to tell you that when life hands you lemons you should make lemonade. But the truth is, when life hands you lemons, it's just more sourness.[51] But I do have some helpful tips, starting with this: identify what is keeping you in the funk and stop investing in that.

For example, you know when you feel some sort of odd pain in your body or have a new symptom? You immediately get on WebMD or the

---

51 Use lemons to garnish your cocktail.

Mayo Clinic site. You frantically type in that one thing that's bothering you, and up pops the many possible causes ranging from a paper cut (probably from filling out all the adoption paperwork) to an incurable disease that only 1 in every 1,456,002 people have. Your mind races. You wonder how your partner will survive without you, who will feed your precious cat, what flowers will be at your funeral (because lilies make you gag). It's all very soap opera-esque. Then you think, screw it. I will do whatever I want since I have limited days. I will eat the deep-dish pizza (even though you know what dairy does to your digestive system), I will not care what other people think (sure, honey, keep telling yourself that), and I will tell my mother-in-law exactly what is on my mind the next time she comments on my living room décor (like her mauve and mint living room décor is something to write home about).

There's no need to go this far down the path. If looking at the online profiles of other hopeful parents is revving up envy, stop looking at the profiles. If attending baby showers is chipping away at your heart, politely decline the invitations. If jogging at the park on Saturdays alongside the gobs of parents pushing strollers, jog somewhere else.

Don't stop living life, but do stop torturing yourself.

Another tip is to focus on something new and positive. Whatever that thing is that you've always wanted to learn (photography, knitting, yoga), commit to doing it. Psychologists agree that you cannot take something away (say, your obsession with looking at other hopeful parents' online profile books and comparing yourself to them) and not replace it with something else.

Of course, making these two changes isn't going to eradicate your adoption woes. This is when you need to decide if joining an adoption support group would be helpful. I recommend an in-person group, if possible, because online groups are full of strangers with whom you cannot look into their eyes or offer a hug. There is certainly something lost in online "connections." Futhermore, online interactions are problematic in that they tend to be a whole lot of drama which will only make your funk worse, not better.

If joining a support group isn't possible or isn't healthy for you right now, you can opt to seek professional counseling. But for the love of margaritas, find someone educated on adoption. Nothing is worse than a professional of any kind using outdated adoption terminology, perpetu-ating stereotypes ("God bless you for your willingness to give a child in need such a good home"), and demonizing birth parents.

You have to find what works for you, and then you have to do it. Because what you're doing now is ridiculous, like as ridiculous as the new "skinny" Oreos and Channing Tatum going anywhere with his shirt ON. Silliness. Pure silliness.

Adopting is Like Driving

When the baby is born, do you take new mom a gift? What do you take? Should you ask her about you nursing the baby, and when? Do you co-name the baby? Is it ok to be part of the baby's hospital photo session? Should you have a baby shower for a baby you are matched with? Is it ok to post sonogram pics of your-maybe-future-baby on social media so your friends and family can see?

I'm going to cut to the chase here: when you choose to adopt, you need to stay in your lane.

The issue with veering outside your lane is that such an action can impact many other people in significant ways. There are always consequences for dangerous actions. No veering into oncoming traffic, no weaving in and out, no riding the shoulder or the middle line, no tailgating or distracted driving, no racing, no driving in dangerous conditions.

It's simple, really. Just stay in your lane. Know your place. Keep yourself in check.

This is the absolute easiest way to keep things as simple, and as ethical, as possible. So anytime you have a question, ask yourself, am I staying in my lane?

Sprinkle, Shower, Bath

I n the adoption community, many new and hopeful adoptive parents
want to know: is it OK to have a baby shower?

First, I'm one person with one journey and four children. Here's my
experience and my thoughts. You do what works for you and your situation.

Like many adoptive-moms-to-be, I struggled at times with feelings of
isolation, indifference and frustration. I didn't belong to most "mommy
clubs": the clubs where moms circled around one another and talked about
stretch marks and which features of their children came from their husbands.
But like many mothers, I wanted to be prepared when my baby arrived with
bottles washed, clothing folded, crib put together, and the nursery painted.

One rite-of-passage for moms is the baby shower. Yes, the time when
you open presents for everyone to ooo-and-ahhh! over, eat super-sugary,
pastel-iced cake, and hug great aunts drenched in perfume who ask you
what names you've picked out.

As soon as our homestudy to adopt an infant was complete, a few of
my friends and family members decided to host an "Expecting a Baby"
shower for me. My husband and I eagerly went to a few local department
stores to register. We were asked some basic, initial information, including our baby's due date. Laughable, really. We selected the end of the
year with high hopes[52] and proceeded to get scanner-gun happy on every
adorable, gender-neutral baby item available.

---

52 Fail.

The shower was held on a Saturday afternoon. The hostesses had transformed a church fellowship hall into a pastel-paradise. I was thrilled to not only find our family members filling the seats, but also one of my college professors, past co-workers and friends. Their presence said to me: *we are with you. We love you. And we already love your baby.*

As I sat at the front of the room, surrounded by nearly one-hundred beautifully wrapped boxes, I realized just how incredible adoption is. All of these guests were gathered around me to not only support my decision to become a mommy but to also to welcome an unknown little one with all the necessary material things he or she would need.

I opened gift after gift, posing for photos with tiny green outfits, rubber duckies, soft stuffed animals and homemade blankets. My mother-in-law gave me a onesie that said, "What happens at Grandma's stays at Grandma's." She was ready to spoil a new little one.

There were no silly games like "guess-how-big-mom's-pregnant-stomach-is." There were no predictions of when the baby would be born. But that was OK. Because I knew that I was surrounded by supporters who were eager to meet and come to know our bundle-of-joy-to-be.

A day later, my husband and I returned home and began to unpack the pile of gifts. We placed sleepers in dresser drawers, arranged rows of board books, put together the diaper bin and folded bedding. It was getting real. And because we had a shower, we felt more ready, more authentic. We were going to be parents. Real parents. Legit.[53]

Our first child arrived fourteen months after our baby shower. And though the wait was long and emotionally draining, it was well worth it.

Now, if you're going to have a shower, here are a few suggestions:

1: Don't have the shower for a specific baby you are matched with.
    It's already in the back of your mind: the what ifs. What if this baby doesn't become ours? What if the mom decides to parent?Thus, if you're going to have a shower, have a generic shower for the baby who does come home to you. Don't get the bibs monogrammed or the cake tinged pink or blue. (Plus, we all know chocolate cake with chocolate icing is the best anyway!)

---

53 Too legit to quit.

2: <u>Make adjustments.</u>

I know in many families and circles of friends, showers traditionally involve certain games, activities, and snacks. It is OK to move away from this and make the shower as adoption-friendly as possible. You don't need reminders on your special day that you are an "other" type of mother. Because you aren't. You won't give birth, but in the end, you will have a baby in your arms that will be your "own." I know ladies who have had open-house style showers (so show up anytime between such and such time) with no games. I know ladies who have had their shower where the guests click together champagne glasses (because mama can drink!) and laugh over appetizers. Co-ed showers are increasingly popular (and fun), allowing both parents-to-be to enjoy the celebration. Whatever works, works. Just because showers have "always been this way," doesn't mean they can't use a makeover.

3: <u>Enjoy it.</u>

You absolutely deserve to have a shower and welcome your future little one into your heart and home. You are going to be a real mom to a real baby, and you should relish in that beauty and blessing.

Cheers to you, REM!

REM: Round 2

You don't have an ultrasound picture, but you're choosing a photographer.

You don't have cravings at 10:00 p.m., but you've got baby on the brain 24/7.

You don't have strangers rubbing your belly, but you are tempted to rub the pregnant belly of someone else.[54]

You don't have a due date, but you know you could have the world's longest or shortest "pregnancy" because who knows when your call will come.

You don't get to park in the "new mom" parking space, but you're shopping for a "baby on board" sign for the back window.[55]

You don't have a long "cannot eat these foods list," but you are researching BPA free bottles and organic baby food.

You don't have a mucus plug to lose, but you are putting those safety outlet plugs in every outlet in your home (before the social worker arrives).[56]

---

54 Sometimes you're better off thinking something rather than proceeding to step two: action. Don't try to touch some random pregnant lady with a gaze of longing in your eyes. You might end up in jail. Or at minimum, starring in a viral video.

55 But please don't actually get one. Don't get a stick figure family. Don't get a "my kid is on the honor roll." Just don't. It makes me want to rear end the people who have any of these. Please use your money more wisely. Tacos, for example, is a better way to spend $9.99.

56 Medical stuff doesn't generally freak me out, but who named a mucus plug "mucus plug." It's about as beautiful as the following combinations: moist panties, genital warts, and Home Depot. Blech, blech, blech.

You aren't posting baby bump pics on social media, but you are obsessively looking at other people's baby pics and wondering what your future baby will look like.

You aren't reading *What to Expect When You're Expecting*, but you are reading the first book that applies to you: *What to Expect In the First Year.*[57]

You aren't buying maternity shirts and those weird pants with flesh-toned "panels" in the front, but you are buying onesies for your future bundle of joy.

You aren't answering questions about when you are due and if you're having a girl or a boy, but you do have the privilege of being an adoption educator to every Tom, Dick, and Harry.[58]

You aren't making a birth plan, but you should be making plans.[59]

---

57 Note, these books have sold a bazillion copies and I think can be helpful to know if your child is developmentally behind. However, for the most part, I recommend saving your money for more important things, such as a new wine or the latest issue of *People*. Let's be real. Trashy celeb magazines and alcohol will help you far more than any textbook full of teeny, tiny print about how-to-compare-your-baby-to-other-babies-so-you-get-so-worried-that-you-go-on-anti-anxiety-meds.

58 I don't know where the Tom, Dick, and Harry saying came from, but those names... I recommend investing in a baby naming book (instead of the aforementioned *What to Expect When You're Expecting*) or at minimum, find yourself an honest friend who will remind you that Pineapple Gertrude Rolls Royce isn't a "unique and cool" baby name.

59 Like vacation plans, like plans to learn a new skill or join a book club, like plans to go on a date with your partner. I have warned you that sitting around drumming your fingers on the kitchen table will not make your baby arrive any faster. And don't just make plans, but turn those plans into action.

Hold the Phone[60]

I want to take a minute and let you know that adoption can be so freak-ing overwhelming. I mean, it can send you into full out panic mode: heart racing, hands shaking, lips trembling, carb guzzling. You might readily admit this, and it may be glaringly apparent anyway.

Or you might try to hide it (like I do). I definitely fit into the category of woman with high functioning anxiety. So let me talk to you (and me) by saying this: Don't attempt to minimize the significance. You are add-ing a life, a human being, to your family: forever. You have a lot on the proverbial line. Those little sprinkles of hope (that onesie you had to buy, the empty picture frame, even a copy of this book sitting expectantly on your nightstand) are juxtaposed with reminders of fear (stacks of adoption paperwork, the voicemail icon with the big fat ZERO above it, the empty nursery).

Adopting is HARD. It's heartbreaking. It's scary. It's confusing. It's mind-numbing and mind-racing (at the EXACT same time). Just when you think you're cool, you are "fine" (as you tell people who ask), a reminder of why you are adopting (infertility, disability, disease) slaps you in the face. You can practically see a POW! scroll across your eyes like in an old Batman movie.

Do you ever just want to bury yourself in your comforter and not come out for six days? Do you ever want to belly-flop onto your sofa, letting

---

60 Does anyone say this anymore?

the fabric mold to your body, and then grunt in response to questions, if someone dares to speak to you? How about just lean over your freezer for two weeks straight, spooning ice cream into your mouth? Can anyone hit me up with a Chardonnay IV?

As I write this part of the book, I'm in this place. I promised you in the intro that I'm not some hoity-toity "expert" who has nothing at stake and who sits on my throne of knowledge with a degree in Adoption Superiority with a minor in Research Extraordinaire. Let me tell you where I am right now. We are matched with a baby due in just a few months, and we've already been matched two months. I sometimes think I'm going completely crazy. One minute my heart is flooded with hope: fairy wings, shooting stars, glitter, chocolate snow, cotton candy, and hydrangeas. The next minute, I feel chained to dismay as if my life is nothing but traffic jams, meatloaf with shredded coconut, and endless episodes of *MASH*.[61] Some days I stroll about confidently, a soy latte in my hand, thinking I look like a supermodel and am rocking this mom thing and other days, I muster every bit of courage I can possibly find just to get my rear out of bed, shuffle to the kitchen, and make breakfast for my kids.

I feel like my life right now is one big MAYBE. One big WHAT IF. One big question mark. I'm trying desperately to pray for the expectant mother and father and unborn baby. I'm attempting to be supportive and ethical and kind. But I'm human. Sometimes I have thoughts that are all about ME and my desires. It's an angel-on-one-shoulder, devil-on-the-other kind of thing. It's torturous. I know I'm supposed to lean on Jesus (I mean, I wrote an adoption devotional book! You'd think I'd have this down pat), but sometimes it's just easier to go into my head, letting thoughts entangle themselves like a knock-off Slinky that took a few trips down the staircase.

One second I want to post on social media that I'm a REM[62] followed by twenty exclamation points and celebratory emjois. The next second,

---

61 These are all things I loathe. No, I've never had meatloaf with shredded coconut, but that certainly sounds like an absolutely revolting combination. But if someone wanted to torture me, they'd blow smoke in my face while making me watch *MASH* on a DVD player in an old, scary van while forcing me to eat meatloaf with shredded coconut. You're welcome for the visual!

62 Remember this? Real Expecting Mom, for those of you who were too busy eating ice cream to pay attention to the earlier chapter on REMs.

I am certain that I will never have another child, probably because my thighs aren't very toned, I have adult acne flair ups, I've never watched *Game of Thrones* (don't get that channel), and I think malted milk balls were invented by Satan.[63] I am so unbelievably irrelevant and uncool; therefore, I am absolutely unworthy of mothering.

One day I'm running out of steam. The next day I'm full of abundant energy. What I really need is a bundle of acceptance, grace, and patience dropped down to me via a little beeping parachute like in the *Hunger Games* movies, preferably with a note attached from God about how all this is going to turn out so I can stop being such a damn control freak.

Since there are no beeping parachutes, cotton candy, or Chardonnay IVs in sight, I'm left with this (incomplete) manuscript, my pathetic prayers, my almost-finished baby nursery, and a secret stash of coffee flavored ice cream.

And for today, that's got to be enough. I know I need to be in this moment, enjoying these summer days with my children. I know I need to focus on the path at my feet, and not on tomorrow.[64]

So no. I have no magical solution for your feelings right now, because I don't have it together either. I'm writing this book because one, I know that it's necessary: that someone out there needs some comic relief and a reminder that there is always prayer, wine, and another woman nearby standing in your same vulnerable space. I'm clinging to you in solidarity. This book is my gift to you, and it's therapy for me, so win-win, right? I don't know what tomorrow will bring. I don't even know what the next five minutes will bring. Bless you. Bless me. This is one wild, unpredictable, heart-wrenching journey, and I want you to know that I get exactly what it's like. I feel you.

Shall we continue?

---

63 As if these things have anything to do with adopting and motherhood…I can be a wee bit of a drama mama sometimes. Don't judge me!

64 Matthew 6:34. Yep, I'm a real Bible scholar. Or really just someone who can use Google to look up verses I remember underlining in my NKJV Bible during church camp in high school.

Hurry Up and Wait

I interrupt this semi-well-organized book to tell you that waiting to adopt, especially after being matched, is sheer torture.

Waiting feels like your heart and mental stability are as strong as egg shells in the palms of a three-year-old. You feel like at any moment, things could go really, really well or really, really bad.

When we were waiting for our fourth child, I created a meme with a vintage Wonder Woman toy in the background, the words "waiting to adopt is my superpower" splayed across her chest. Truly, waiting feels like it requires some sort of super, other-worldly, alien strength.

You must walk through the pain, and it's OK and healthy to admit, that waiting is hard.

Here's the dealy-o. If you are so set on avoiding pain or dismissing it, that heartset and mindset is not healthy now, and it's really not healthy when you are parenting a child who very well might express hard feelings surrounding his or her adoption. If you immunize yourself by whatever means you deem appropriate and necessary, you will continue to do so, teaching your child that admitting and discussing and sharing pain isn't OK.

I reject the notion that you should be fine because you are the one who will, at the end of the process, end up with your dreams coming true. I refuse to believe that you shouldn't be honest with yourself about the challenges of waiting because someone else is hurting. I won't deny myself permission to be in the seasons of hardship because I'm too busy contemplating all the reasons why other people are telling me I shouldn't struggle.

To thine own self be true, my friends.

It doesn't mean you don't have empathy for others. It doesn't mean you aren't educated on adoption. It doesn't mean you're unethical.

It just means you're human.

When it's Yes, Then No

Many, many hopeful parents experienced "failed" adoptions. The definition of failed adoption is fluid. It might mean you were matched with a mama who didn't place. It might mean you brought a baby into your home and heart, legal-risk, and the baby ended up with his biological father. It might mean hearing "no" (seemingly) one thousand times when your profile was shown and feeling your heart shatter, again. It might mean you were gung-ho to adopt, but your partner began wavering and said, "I'm not ready." It might mean putting your adoption plans on hold when you found out you were pregnant.

Adoptions "fail" in many ways, and no matter how the cookie crumbles (I'm obsessed with cookies), it is completely devastating. Your family's future is on the line. Your dreams, your yearnings, your heart.

During our first adoption journey, our profile was shown ten to fifteen times. Honestly, I lost count. Because at first, I was over-the-moon. Showing? WHOO HOO! This could be THE one. Nope. Once the cycle repeated itself a few times, I surrendered to the reality that I had zero control and should probably just buy expensive ice cream and eat my feelings. We were bound for a bumpy ride, one with no established "due date."

One day our social worker called to tell us an expectant mother in Michigan wanted to meet us. We were thrilled and scared. We booked a hotel, planned a date to travel, and then spent the next few weeks "dieting" (AKA: not eating because we were so nervous and anxious). Two days before we were to leave to meet her, the social worker called. Mom was in pre-term labor, and the thought of losing her baby made her decide she absolutely needed parent him. The medical scare was her wakeup call that her baby boy needed her, and her mama bear kicked in.

A few months later, the social worker called again. An expectant mother in Hawaii was considering placing her baby with us. Hawaii? My mind (I am a writer, you know) went to sandy beaches, balmy breezes, and fruity drinks. We got to wait out ICPC in Hawaii while bonding with our new baby on a beach? Um, yes! But the communication between the social worker and the expectant mom gradually disappeared, and we were left deflated. Again.

Of course, we were very happy these moms chose what was best for their babies. We prayed fervently for them: that they would have resources, courage, and conviction. That they were happily parenting. But it didn't stop us from feeling all the feels that come with a broken heart.

In two of our four adoptions, there were moments when we were very, very uncertain if the placements would happen. I'm keeping those details private (just as I've told you to keep the details of your child's story private!): but I will tell you, I have never been so anxious in my entire life. Not because I thought I deserved the baby. Not because I wanted a mom to go against her mommy-gut. Not because I'm a selfish B. But because my life, my heart, my dream of mommyhood was hanging by a thread.

There's just no easy way out. No heart protection. Choosing to adopt means choosing to have your heart broken, often many, many times. And all I can tell you, as someone one the "other side," is that every time there's a "no" or a "failure," you are building up to the moment your answer will be "yes" and "forever."

So hang on, sister. This is the ride of your life. There is going to be heartache, big questions, and even bigger feelings. This is the journey, one thousands of us have already traveled. And one day, you will join the ranks of the motherhood-by-adoption.

The Tie that Binds

When a baby's umbilical cord is cut, there is a swift break between mother and child. If that baby is placed for adoption, the separation is much more drastic. Baby moves from a familiar voice, heartbeat, and scent, as well as in-utero environment, to a brand-new person with a different voice, heartbeat, scent, and, of course, environment.

In the adoption community the idea of the primal wound is controversial. The premise is that an adoptee (remember, that's a child who was adopted) faces a traumatic loss (ongoing) due to being separated from his or her biological parent(s). Some adoptees firmly believe in the primal wound, while others do not.

I'm not here to argue if the primal wound is real or not, as that's not my place, but I do want to provide you with some avenues in which you can help your new baby get acclimated to you, known as bonding, so that the child and you can form a secure attachment.

What the heck is attachment anyway? From listening to attachment therapists, to reading several books (including the very best: *The Connected Child: Bring Hope and Healing to your Adoptive Family*), to conversations with triad members, and being in attachment support groups, I have gathered that the attachment a child has with his or her parents is the foundation in which all other relationships and attachments are built. Thus, if the child has a positive and solid attachment to his or her parents, future relationships are far more likely to be healthy and successful.

There are many ways new parents may opt to bond with their child with the goal of positive, strong, and healthy attachment. Some possibilities include:

Adoptive nursing. Nursing a baby you adopt is more common than ever before. There are several options including inducing lactation (making your own milk); nursing a baby through a supplemental feeding system with your own milk, donor milk, or formula; bottle nursing (feeding baby via a bottle with his or her face against your bare chest); comfort nursing (also known as "dry nursing"). There is no right or wrong answer, and if you opt to feed your baby with formula through a bottle, that's OK too. I had the opportunity to comfort nurse one of my children for several months, and it was an incredibly meaningful and special experience for us. Nursing, whether you make milk or not, is a means of bonding: eye contact, skin-to-skin, time spent together, etc. I highly recommend that you read Alyssa Schnell's book *Breastfeeding Without Birthing* if you want to learn more about adoptive nursing.

Baby wearing. Baby wearing is pretty self-explanatory, isn't it? In essence, you find a baby carrier you like, and you "wear" your baby. The close contact, much like nursing, promotes bonding. Baby wearing creates a womb-like experience for the child. There are many, many baby carrier brands and types. It's helpful for new moms (and dads!) to join baby wearing groups that can offer support in selecting a carrier, proper use of the carrier, and encouragement. I wore each of my babies for different lengths of time, including wearing my son until he was over age three.

Co-sleeping. Co-sleeping again promotes closeness between parent and child. However, safe co-sleeping practices are incredibly important. There are many options and tips available. If you don't wish to co-sleep, you can always keep the baby in your bedroom for as long as you feel necessary. This way you are able to quickly respond to baby's cries and whimpers.

Cocooning. Cocooning is most common in the case of an international adoption; however, some parents who have adopted children domestically have also taken part in the practice. Basically, the parent or parents shut themselves in their home with their child for a certain amount of time, being the only ones who feed, cuddle, change, and bathe the baby. This time of intimacy is used to bond and create a secure attachment. An alternative is to agree, as parents, to be the only ones to care for the baby, but not necessarily quarantine themselves in their home. They allow other people to hold the baby or see the baby, but they do all the parental tasks.

Many of these practices are common in what is known as attachment parenting. I know for some, attachment parenting brings to mind tree hugging, weed smoking, sandal wearing parents who nurse babies until they are seven, but today's attachment parent could be you: a parent-by-adoption who wants to approach parenting their new baby with intentionality in order to create secure attachment.

No matter what you decide, it's important to be responsive to your mommy-gut. What does THIS particular baby need given his or her circumstances including physical health? Take it day-by-day and step-by-step. You'll get your sea legs.

The Day You're Handed Someone Else's/Your Baby

The day we met our first child was certainly memorable.

We had been painting our kitchen a few days prior when my husband's cell phone rang. He didn't recognize the number, but being the Mr. Curious he is, picked it up. His eyes grew wide, and then he thrust the phone at me.

It was THE call.

The social worker asked us if we'd like our profile shown for a baby girl already born. We said yes and then spent two hours feeling like we were going to vomit. In a daze, we cleaned up our paint mess, changed, and headed to the high school play a friend was directing. About five minutes into our drive, the phone rang again.

Chosen.

And just like that, we were parents.

Fast forward a few days. We arrive in Kansas City with our car full of baby stuff. We meet our social worker at our hotel, sign some papers, and then follow her into the rush-hour traffic. Minutes seem like years. Finally we arrive at a sprawling home with a beautiful garden stone in the front that boasted of "Heaven's Baby Lodge." (We later learned our child was the 173rd baby to be cared for by Mama Kay and Daddy Mike.) We walked up the steps, our hearts pounding.

The door eased open, and there stood Mama Kay with a five pound baby in her arms. She smiled at me and said, "She's hungry and poopy, Mom."

Holy moly. I was "Mom."

The next day, we went to court to gain custody of our daughter. It was a deeply emotional day, knowing one mom was surrendering and another mom was gaining.

It can take some time to feel like the mother to a child that comes to you by adoption. Or it can be instantaneous love. Or something in between. There is no right or wrong, good or bad. Each adoption is different. Each child is different. Each mother is different. More on this in another chapter.

It's important to accept the moment for what it is, embrace the emotions (no matter how minimal or overwhelming), and be intentional about bonding. And remember, if and until TPR is signed and the revocation period is over, the baby is THEIRS, not YOURS.

The shift from hers-to-yours is major. It's abrupt and overwhelming. There might be some big emotions in that shift, including sadness for the baby's first parents colliding with your joy. There's nothing quite like this moment in your family's story. It is one of both overwhelming relief and struggle.

Whatever you feel, it is not right or wrong, normal or abnormal. This is your process, this is your journey, these are your emotions, and you've just got to work through them.

In essence, girl! You are a mommy! Congrats. Celebrate. Take 1,000,000 pictures every day (every hour!). Relish in these precious moments, because the old ladies who stop you at the grocery store are right: it goes by so fast.

It's My Party and I'll Cry If I Want to

his chapter is short and sweet. And very necessary.

The day you are placed with a baby who will be yours forever, your emotions may take you by surprise.

I'm sure you're anticipating joy, elation, and gratitude. But what you may not know is that these feelings may collide with sadness, uncertainty, and even guilt.

When you become a mom to a baby you didn't birth, a baby who doesn't share your DNA, a baby who was placed with you instead of grown within you, polarizing emotions collide. And here's why: because you recognize that another woman's loss is your gain. You realize that you wouldn't be a mom without the sacrifice of another. And this is very, very difficult to process. And it's good. Because if you are having big emotions, you have a heart for your child's birth family and for your child.

So this is my permission slip to you: if, when your baby arrives, you feel conflicted, good. Work through every high and low, every ounce of happiness and pain. Feel the weight of it all. Surrender to all that comes organically. Because in doing so, you are being a good mom to your baby.

Once Upon a Time: When Everybody Wants to Know the Story

Some adoptions are more apparent than others. If your adoption is transracial, if you live in a community where everyone knows everyone, or you adopted twins when you were obviously not pregnant, you are going to get a lot of questions about your new little(s). You'll be asked, as we often are, very personal details about your child's story.

Let me be clear about this: though you and your child's stories are intricately woven, the adoption story ultimately belongs to your child, not you.

Therefore, if you take something personal and sacred and begin tearing off little pieces to hand out, what might that mean in the future? What might that do to your relationship with your child? What if someone tells your child a part of their story before you do?

One thing that I've noticed with a lot of women is that we are programmed (by our parents, by our church, by our teachers, by society in general) to be polite, accommodating, and cooperative. When something is asked of us, we should pony up.

Before you keep reading, I want you go to listen to Miranda Lambert's song "Mama's Broken Heart." Don't argue. Even if you don't like country music, you need to hear this song. Now go!

If you gave the song proper attention, you get the message loud and clear: there's so much pressure on women to keep it together and make sure that no one around them is uneasy. It doesn't matter what storm the woman is navigating; she needs to keep her shit together.

Now, I'm not saying that when random stranger #34 is asking you, "Why didn't her birth parents keep her?" you should go ballistic like you're in an episode of the *Real Housewives* where your so-called bestie, in a drunken haze, tried to seduce your married brother. But there is nothing wrong with prioritizing the sacred relationship between you and child over Mrs. Unibrow's desire to get "the scoop."[65]

When someone gets up in your business, someone who has no right to be in your business, you can do a few things:

- Change the subject.
- Ignore.
- Walk away.
- Say, "That's private" or "We keep that information in our family."
- Hand over a business card from your adoption professional and say, "It sounds like you want to know more about adoption."

I've said it before, and I'll say it again. Do not hand out your child's adoption story like a grandma hands out cookies.[66]

---

65 Simply typing about a creepy stranger encounter makes me want to eat some mint chip.
66 You knew I'd keep bringing carbs into this conversation, didn't you? Good girl! You've been paying attention!

Grandma's Cookies

Recently a reader of mine submitted a new burning adoption question regarding privacy. *Why do you keep my children's names, faces, and stories private?*

In a time when ever'body knows ever'body else's business and divulging increases the popularity of bloggers, why do I stay in the shadows? What am I so afraid of? What am I hiding?

As a mom of four kids, all of whom have open adoptions with their birth families, I feel like we've had reunions on a much smaller (but no less meaningful) scale: every visit is sacred and special. Every laugh. Every question. Every matching smile (because WOW is the "nature" evident and so beautiful!).

Never. Ever. Ever would it be ok to exploit or broadcast these moments.

Yet I see it all the time. The mom posting a pic of her transracial adoptee on IG with the hashtag #HIVCantStopHer. The hopeful adoptive parent posting a picture of the baby she's matched with: the baby IN UTERO, like yes, in the expectant mother's uterus. These are just two appalling examples. There are those who refer to the expectant mom (they are matched with) as "our birth mother" and the baby (yep, the one in utero) as "our baby girl or "our baby boy."

Though I do share things that happen to our family, such as when my toddler was called a thug by an acquaintance, or when I was referred to, yet again, as my kids' "adoptive" mom, I do not share my children's names, faces, or personal adoption stories. I don't share the names and faces of their birth families either.

Why?

- Because it's not for public consumption.
- Because it's not your business.
- Because it's not my story to tell.
- Because privacy matters. Privacy translates to respect. Respect is a way of loving.
- Because I don't trust strangers with intimate things.
- Because anything online can never be erased.
- Because I want to live a life with as few regrets as possible.
- Because I take my job as a mother very seriously.
- Because I believe in respecting my children's biological families and their stories.
- Because I was chosen to parent my children, and this honor shouldn't be squandered.
- Because I know many adoptees and birth families: and listening to them tells me it's better to err on the side of caution and privacy.
- Because no amount (fleeting) praise is worth compromising my relationship with my children. (And I did not adopt to be praised.)
- Because I didn't save my children.
- Because I am the lucky one.

I have been asked many times, by prominent people and networks, to submit photos of my kids' faces, share their names, or allow them to speak on camera or radio. And my answer is always no. No, I cannot answer that question. No, I will not share why my children were placed for adoption. No, you can't have a photo of my children. No, they won't be speaking on camera.

Not because my children's voices do not matter, but because their voices matter the MOST.

We are not ashamed of the fact that our family was built by adoption. But we hold some things sacred because otherwise, they are thrown like confetti to the masses. Obliterating their holiness.

I want to encourage you to think about the potential long-term implications of your immediate choices. Things like who you share your child's story with. Things like the language you use to explain adoption. Things like the questions you choose to answer. Things like privacy. The pictures and videos you share. The things you agree to.

You, as your child's parent, have so much power and influence and responsibility. Adoption and parenting adoptees is NOT about warm fuzzies, fame, personal satisfaction.

It's about raising happy, confident, empowered children. It's about listening to them. Empathizing. Learning and applying. Teaching and guiding. Leading by example. And that starts on the foundation of trust. Trust is everything.

One of the things I tell parents-by-adoption all the time is this: Don't hand out your child's story, or parts of their stories, like a grandma hands out cookies. It's that simple.

The Babysitter's Club

W hen I was in grade school, I was completely obsessed with Sweet Valley and Babysitter's Club books. (Who wasn't?) Then came *Saved by the Bell*. Preteen and teenage angst was everything. Many of the uh-oh moments stemmed from babysitting.[67]

When you adopt, you may feel like the child's babysitter for a while. You do the things (bathing, feeding, diapering, cuddling, comforting), you take the pictures, and you genuinely like the child, but sometimes you just aren't in the Love Department yet. Going from "like" to "love" can take days, weeks, or even months. This is normal.

But what about when your adoption is pretty open, and you know that one major factor in not falling head-over-heels for your baby is that you are drinking from the continuous cocktail of guilt and obligation to the child's birth family? This is more likely in the case of a more open adoption. Perhaps you were matched with the birth family for weeks or even months before the child's birth: back when the baby was just "the baby" and not your baby. Back when the baby was in utero, your energy and focus was solely with the birth family.

When a baby is born and TPR is signed and official, your obligation and allegiance takes an abrupt shift from birth mother to baby. This shift happens whether you desire it or not. When you are handed a baby (sometimes without much advanced planning), that baby (like all babies) is

---

67 Remember that episode of *Full House* when DJ and Stephanie were fighting and plunged a closet pole into the wall of their dad's bedroom? Oops…

reliant solely on you to do absolutely everything for him or her. And this is exhausting and time consuming. Suddenly you have less time and energy for the birth family (and really, for anyone in your life).

I've seen it shared many times: a woman struggles to feel like "mom" because of the intense level of openness in the adoption. Birth mom and new mom may have a very strong bond, and of course, they share a son or daughter. When new mom is suddenly overwhelmed by the responsibility of caring for the baby, complexity erupts like volcano.

New mom feels that if she lessens communication with birth mom, she is a bad person. She may feel that staying closely connected with birth mom will help ease some of birth mom's grief or calm her anxieties about placing. New mom wants to soothe her own guilt about parenting another woman's baby.

It's an awkward, tender, fragile dance, and there are no easy answers.

This is what I can tell you from my experience, from having four open adoptions, all of which started with the placement of brand-new babies. Let's start with what your jobs are:

- To care for yourself. Cliché but true: you cannot give what you do not have. If you are neglecting your own needs, it will wear you down and take a toll on your relationships, your health, and your ability to best care for your baby.
- To care for your baby. Duh. You need to be bonding with your baby, meeting your baby's needs, and learning all about your new little one. Revisit the chapter on attachment practices.
- To care for your partner. This is the person you've pledged to love for life, the fellow parent to your new child, and your teammate.
- To care for your other children, if any. If you're already parenting, you have an obligation to them. Help them adjust to having a new sibling in the home while also spending one-on-one time with them, meeting their individual needs.

Your job is not:

- To be your child's birth parents' counselor. You are way too close to the situation to be the one the birth parent confesses all their thoughts and feelings and struggles too.

- **To be your child's birth parents' parent.** Sometimes when a younger mom and dad place a baby for adoption, they are seeking a surrogate parental figure. They look up to the parents who adopted the child. Perhaps their own parents weren't "good" parents or supportive of the adoption plan, but you are supportive and loving.
- **To be your child's birth parents' advisor or rescuer.** There's a difference between offering suggestions and encouragement when asked and relentlessly working to "fix" someone. You cannot live your life to meet their every need, demand, or cry for help.

It's a fine line. You can be supportive, encouraging, and loving without crossing a boundary. I urge you not to try to play dual roles. Mainly because it's not ethical. And yes, ethics matter, even after the placement. Ever heard of the phrase "spread too thin"? By taking on responsibilities you were never meant to have, you will spread yourself too thin and something is bound to break. Who does this hurt the most? The child you were chosen to parent! The result? You are expending so much time and energy to others instead of focusing on bonding with your baby. So yep, you're going to feel like a babysitter!

Again, remember this, especially if you and/or the birth family are new to adoption: relationships are always challenging and adoption is new. It's ok for anyone to make mistakes, to struggle, to fumble. Open adoption requires many things, and this includes patience, grace, forgiveness, encouragement, and commitment.

And you don't get to be a flake when things get difficult. This is not one of those situations where "if you can't stand the heat, get outta the kitchen." Friend, it's going to get hot. It's going to get hot when a friend announces her pregnancy, and you're thrust back into THAT place where you grapple with jealousy even though you have a beautiful baby in your arms. It's going to get hot when birth mom expresses her grief and hints that she regrets placing. It's going to get hot when your text messages go unreturned for weeks on end.

Let me be clear: we've had many ups and downs in our open adoptions. We juggle the responsibility of raising four children and maintaining healthy relationships with four birth families, all of whom are very different from one another. There have been times things were "too close for comfort," and we had to make changes in our open adoptions in order to make sure that our children were our top priority. These were HARD choices. These were heartbreaking moments. But I can look back with confidence and say we did the right things, in the right time, with the right heart-set, keeping our children as our number one priority.

Remember, you were chosen to raise this child for a reason. And you need to continue in that responsibility with courage and conviction. This is not the time to be a doormat, a wimp, or a whiner. And it's also not the time to bail because feelings of jealousy, confusion, uncertainty, or frustration crop up. This chapter is not your permission slip to back out on your promises.

You are not Claudia, or Mary Anne, or Jessi, or any of those other fabulous girls who filled my fifth grader after-school hours with their baby-sitting dilemmas. You are Mom, and you need to move beyond acting like one to actually being one.

Singin' the Blues

Feeling blue before and during an adoption is normal. But feeling blue after? Yep, can be normal too. And here's why you're possibly feeling this way:

- Your adoption journey was (and perhaps still is) incredibly tumultuous: failed adoptions, conflict with the birth family, a bad experience with an adoption professional, financial hardship, etc.
- You're adapting to having a baby. Babies are exhausting.
- You're helping your partner and/or other kids adjust to the change in family dynamic.
- You have less time and energy for your partner, your other children, other relationships, your interests, your job, etc.
- You're still in legal risk with the adoption: maybe the birth father didn't terminate his rights/cannot be found/is unknown, maybe you live in a state where there's a revocation period (in which the baby's biological parents can decide to parent), etc.
- You're experiencing many changes at once, especially in your usual routine.
- You're dreading the upcoming changes such as the end of your maternity leave.
- Your baby had a rough start (NICU stay, for example) and/or continued health issues.

- You are feeling the pressure of being an "adoptive" parent. You are constantly asked questions and feel as though you must be a super mom.

A major issue for many is that that you are expected by others (and possibly by yourself also) to be overjoyed that you are finally a mom. This leaves little room for any other feelings or thoughts. Any sadness, frustration, exhaustion, confusion shouldn't exist...yet it often does.

Post Adoption Depression is real, recognized in *The Post-Adoption Blues: Overcoming the Unforeseen Challenges of Adoption* by Karen J. Foli and John R. Thompson. Now the book reads much like a textbook, and I don't think you need to read the entire thing to know if you are truly depressed or not. Post Adoption Depression is not completely different from Post-Partum Depression: it's depression resulting from the addition of a baby to the family, but with the babies coming to the families in different ways. Arguably, though you may not have hormones surging and your lady-bits to ice, you are dealing with the typical adjustments in addition to adoption challenges.

If you are singing the blues after you've adopted, which can happen just days after, months, or even years after a placement, you need to seek professional help and get into an adoption support group. There is too much at stake to brush off. Post-Adoption Depression can affect your physical health, your relationships with your partner, friends, and family, and of course, your relationship with your child. Take this in, friend: a lack of self-care is selfish, not selfless.

If you haven't yet adopted, I encourage you to at least skim the book and have an understanding of what PAD is. You may not experience Post-Adoption Depression, but if you do see hints of it after placement, you have the assurance of being proactive rather than simply reactive.

(Not-So) Epic Battle: Nature vs. Nurture

Many choose to adopt a newborn because they want the infant-hood experience. (Wait…they do know that that means months without sleep, right?) They also desire to have a "blank slate" vs. an older child who has more of a history.

Here's the deal: a baby isn't a blank slate to be written upon or a ball of clay to be molded.

When an infant is born, if full-term, has already existed for nearly ten months and was conceived by two people whose genes joined together. Every baby is made up of both nature and nurture: a beautiful blend.

This will be hard to see until your child is in your arms and begins to grow up. Then you will notice: that laugh, the shape of their nose, the sound of their voice. These things will remind you of the child's birth family. It is at times, uncanny, like the day my daughter met her older biological brother for the first time. All of us parents were chit-chatting, our backs to the kids, when we heard one of them laugh. We turned and realized that we couldn't tell which child it was: because they laugh exactly the same. That's two children, raised in two different (adoptive) homes, hundreds of miles apart, with the same indistinguishable laugh.

Later that day, after the kids had played together, the brother's mother and I were sitting on the living room floor together. Our children joined us, each plopping into our laps, their bare feet touching. Simultaneously, we noticed that the children had the exact same feet: tall and wide. We laughed about how we had to buy special, expensive shoes that would fit their foot shape.

These are just two examples of hundreds. The nature part is undeniable. And truly, it's incredible. As is the nurture.

For example, one day my sister and her husband were visiting, and my oldest daughter walked up and said something sassy and then stood there waiting for my sister to respond. My sister exclaimed, "You are standing exactly like your mom did when she was a kid!" I looked over and she was right! My daughter had my pose down to the centimeter! Both my daughter and I are oldest children and have a sense of leadership (some may call it bossiness), determination, and passion.

I think the important thing is that as parents, we accept and love our children for exactly who they are. They did come from other parents, their first/birth parents, and they will be similar in certain ways. But our children are also raised by us, and they pick up on our family environment, our mannerisms and vernacular, the intonations in our voices, and obviously, the way we choose to hold our bodies.

There is no need for a competition between us (the parents who adopted) and them (the biological parents). We are forever intertwined, whether or not the adoption is open, semi-open, or closed. The sooner you embrace the reality, the better.

The Truth Will Set You Free

see it all the time, at least weekly, in Facebook groups. A new parent asks: *When do I tell my child that she is adopted? How do I tell him he's adopted?*

The answer to the "when" is very simple: from the very, very beginning.

There are a few reasons for this. For one, the more you, as the parent, talk to your child about adoption, the more comfortable you become. This prepares you for future conversations where you share more details with your child, answer hard questions, and offer empathy, love, and acceptance. The second reason, and the most important, is that your child deserves to know his or her story. This is true even of a young child.

The answer to the "how" is pretty simple too.

You read age-appropriate adoption books to your child. You create a lifebook, outlining his or her story, and read it just as you would any other story book. You put pictures of your child's birth family in visible places, using those as a catalyst for conversations. You surround your family with other families-by-adoption. If you're a family who prays, include your child's birth family in your bedtime prayers.

As your child gets older, more mature, and more inquisitive, you add more details to the story. You always answer the questions honestly. And when struggles come up that are beyond your abilities in that moment, you seek professional help for you and/or your child.

Now, if you're reading this and you've waited to tell your child, because of insecurities or fears, you may ask, "But now what?" You find a professional to help guide you through the process of talking to your child.

And what if the truth isn't pretty? In adoption, the truth isn't usually pretty. Placements happen because the child's birth parent(s) wasn't in a good circumstance or situation. Some stories are harder than others, but an adoption story is never "easy." A tough story is not an excuse for a parent to deflect, lie, or hide.

We should not assume that by doing all the "right things," our children will not struggle as adoptees. Each child, each adoption, is different. We aren't telling our kids the truth in order to preserve our own pride and hearts. We aren't telling them the truth in an effort to make life perfect. We are telling them the truth because that's the right thing to do. And when challenges arise in the future, we have already established a relationship based on trust, love, acceptance, authenticity, and empathy that will carry us through hard times.

I always remind my children when a sticky situation arises it is important to tell the truth. Because doing the right, good, ethical, fair thing usually yields good results.

Quit Shouting, Sing Louder

E ver since I started school, I wanted to be athletic. But it just wasn't in me.

In third grade, when it was my turn to kick during a PE kickball game, I missed. Every. Single. Time. And in fifth grade dodge-ball, I was the tall, skinny girl who couldn't catch or throw, so I just stood in the game awkwardly until I was the only one left. The kids tried to cheer for me to hit the player on the other team, the person I was terrified of because I feared the rubber ball leaving his tight grip and smacking me in the face. So I just cowered while my teammates starting cheering for the OTHER guy to get me out so we could start the game over already.

When I got to middle school, I still wanted to be an athlete, so I considered cheerleading. All the cool girls were cheerleaders. Yet, I had no tumbling classes under my belt, no strength, and very little confidence.

So in eighth grade, I decided to go to volleyball tryouts. I spent the day before tryouts practicing with a BASKETBALL in my front yard. Can you imagine a basketball hitting the bony forearms of an eighth grader who had yet to even think about starting puberty? It was frigid outside, but I practiced for hours.

I made the team. (I'm guessing there were no cuts.) And I was deemed captain of the "C" team. Yes, as in there was an A team, a B team, and then a C team. I was in charge of the sixth graders. I finally had what I wanted: a uniform, a position, a team-name, teammates, and some sort of prestige among my peers.

As we headed to our first game, cramped on a school bus, the coach stood and gave us a talk. Part of the lecture was about winning and losing. If we win, she said, we could have snacks after the game and cheer and carry on victoriously. If we lost, we should travel home in a somber mood: no talking, cheering, or giggling.

This was so strange to me. I grew up in a loud, opinionated, vocal family. There were five of us. My dad was a disc jockey and salesperson. My mom stayed at home with us. My sister had a "verbal diarrhea" issue prompting my mom to constantly tell her, just because you think something doesn't mean you should say it. My sister and I argued relentlessly, mostly because of our shared bedroom space in which I was tidy and she hid cheese-balls and chocolate under her bed. Yet we were best friends. My little brother was the rope between our tug-of-war and was always at the mercy of our antics.

In essence: we said what we thought. We talked a lot. My mom used to say all she wanted for any holiday gift was "peace and quiet."

The coach was telling me HOW to respond to something. It made no sense to me. Was this what it meant to be on a team? We had to be unified in everything, directed by an adult? We weren't free to have our own reaction? Our own emotions? Our own opinions?

It felt like oppression. That someone was moving into my sacred space and trying to conquer. It didn't sit well with me: not out of rebellion or lack of respect for the coach. (I was terrified of breaking rules.) I was just uneasy about the whole thing, but in my middle-schooler mind, couldn't pinpoint why.

That was twenty-one years ago. And this captain of the volleyball C team hasn't shaken that lecture.

When I see the many, many posts from new parents-by-adoption and those hoping to adopt, I remember that bus ride. These current and hopeful parents ask and ponder:

- What if my child wants to call his or her birth parents "mom" and "dad"?
- I'm not comfortable with visits. We want to stick with just pictures and letters.
- I don't want my child to be confused.
- I can't wait for our child to have once-a-week visits with his birth mom.

- Should I tell my child that she was conceived by rape?
- When should I tell my child his adoption story?

Parents: here's the deal. It's up to us to reveal all the information, as age-and-developmentally appropriate, to our children. It's not up to us to dictate their reactions or shape their stories in a way that's more "gentle" (aka: concealing details). We are to be authentic, forthcoming, and proactive. We are to be truth-tellers, empathy-servants, and hug-dealers.

We should also be space-givers. By that I mean, give our children the space to process and to react as they feel is appropriate. We shouldn't try to mold the outcomes to make ourselves feel better. It's not about us. We shouldn't tamper with the evidence, so to speak.

We have the obligation and the privilege to give our children what we know. It is not up to us, as the coach did to me, dictate the child's response to the events that have already taken place.

There are thousand decisions you will make as a parent surrounding the child's adoption. Questions that need answers. Answers that prompt more questions. Confusion. Joy. Wondering. Peace. All of these. None of these. Some of these.

There's no perfect way to navigate. Though I know many post to Facebook groups seeking to find the no-fail answers to their burning questions. Often when questions are asked, the parent already knows the right thing to do, or the wrong thing that should be avoided. The goal in parenting (by adoption or biology) is not perfection. The goal should be to demonstrate the things that make us good, that enable us to process the things life throws our way and respond to others: empathy, kindness, honesty, encouragement, and, of course, abundant love.

And if there is a "do not" to be shared, it's this: do not tell your child, or expect of your child, to handle adoption in any certain way. A way that makes you more comfortable or proud. A way that doesn't ignite jealousy. A way that makes you let out a breath of relief. Your focus is on your child. You demonstrate authenticity in disclosure, teaching your child that your home is a safe space for authenticity to take root and grow.

You can do this. Your child needs you to be ready with an open mind, heart, and arms, no matter how he or she responds.

Today's Special: Humble Pie

Tell me I'm not the only one who does this.

I go to the grocery store armed with my coupons, reusable bags, and a long list. (I'm usually accompanied by at least one of my four children.)

I get all the groceries, filling the cart. Then I zig-zag around the store with rapidly decreasing energy at least two more times for everything I forgot or skipped before.

I make it to the checkout. I slide the items on the conveyor belt while asking one or two of the children NOT to touch the gum packets and trashy magazines. The cashier rings everything up, I hand over my coupons, and then I pay. Then the moment comes.

"Would you like help out to your car?" asks the person who bagged my groceries.

Before the question is even fully uttered, I interrupt with a clear, loud, and insistent, "No, thanks."

Then I smile (see how confident I am?), and push my cart forward... slowly. Because I'm trying to edge kids to the door while pushing a really, really freaking heavy grocery cart into a bumpy parking lot (usually in the rain, because why would it NOT spontaneously rain when I go to buy groceries?).

When we make it to the minivan, there's the struggle of trying to use the automatic doors WHILE children are pulling on door handles. Once the kids are safely inside the van, I open the trunk to place the groceries inside only to find that I forgot to remove the stroller that takes up the entire trunk space. So then I'm left stuffing groceries in whatever crevice I can find while the rain pours down upon me. I shove the empty cart into the adjoining cart corral and jump into the driver's seat of the van.

Wet. Irritated. Tired.

But I will not be deterred.

When I get home, I tell the kids to go inside, and I proceed to attempt to carry every single grocery bag, no matter how heavy or how full or how fragile the bag is, into the house ALL AT ONCE. Because why in the world would I make two trips from my van, which is just two steps away from the door into the house?

Why? Why not accept the grocery bagger's offer? Why not unload the car bag by bag versus all at once?

It's called stubbornness, and efficiency, and a whole lot of other things. But it's all just pride in a bad disguise. And it's ridiculous.

I'm active in the adoption community and have a decade of education and experience under my belt. I see it time and time and time again: the DIY hopeful parent or mama-by-adoption (already parenting) who wants to do it all herself.

Sure, she'll post an occasional question in an adoption Facebook group full of strangers. But she's pretty much flying solo, because she's spent SO long trying to become a mom. She doesn't want to rely on anyone to do something for her or on her behalf.

I talk about this in my first book *Come Rain or Come Shine: A White Parent's Guide to Adopting and Parenting Black Children*, in chapter three: Super Parent Syndrome. In short, parents who adopt are put on a pedestal (by themselves, their agency, the birth parents, friends and family, strangers, the media, etc.) which puts SO MUCH PRESSURE on them to be everything. This leads to pride.

And remember that thing about pride? It goeth before the fall. (According to Proverbs 16:18.)

How many times have you successfully carried in all the groceries at once without damaging at least one item? Without a bag breaking? Without banging into a nearby wall? Without feeling the pull of your arm muscles and the ache in your back, not just in that moment, but probably the next day, too?

Friend! You WERE NEVER MEANT TO DO THIS ALONE.

When a Black mom approaches you and offers a suggestion for your daughter's hair, consider. When an adoptee tells you that isolating your child of color in an all-White community is dangerous for his well-being, listen. When a birth mother you meet is aching for a photo of her biological child and you remember you forgot to send an update to your child's birth parent last month, take note.

Stop hesitating and re-positioning yourself on the pedestal. Find your child a mentor. Go to the adoption support group meeting. Read the book.

It boils down to humility. Do the stuff.

It's all for your child who depends on you to make the right choices, do the right things, meet and invite the right people into your inner circle.

Yes, agreeing to let someone else help with the "heavy lifting" is going to require some bravery. But the trade-off is peace, empathy, wisdom, and hope.

What's the alternative? Remember, Proverbs warns us that pride = destruction. And the first step is choosing pride. If we elect to dance with pride, we will inevitably engage in destruction.

You've been chosen to parent your child, for whatever reason. It is an honor, a privilege, and a serious task. It's a blessing. Be brave. Have courage. Get off the damn pedestal, no matter whom or what put you on it, then kick the thing over. Break it up with a big hammer. Sweep away the shattered pieces.

And then embrace the joy of having open hands, ready to receive the assistance that is waiting for you.

Middle School Cheers

W hen you adopt you will be asked ridiculous and rude questions. I know that many (usually those outside the adoption community) chalk these questions up to "curiosity."

After a decade in the adoption community, most of that time being a mother, I want to tell you something important: it is not your obligation to educate others on adoption, especially not at the expensive of your children's well-being and privacy.

There are certain people who should know some details of your child's story. Certainly, a doctor needs to know your child's medical history. Certainly, your child's teacher needs to know that your child is an adoptee, because certain assignments like creating the "family tree" might be modified to a family orchard. Certainly, your nearest-and-dearest, your closest friends and family members, will be privy to more details of your child's story because they love and care for your child and will help support and encourage him or her. Notice how few people are listed? That's because, as I've said before, you shouldn't hand out your child's adoption story like a grandma hands out cookies.

Here's a sampling of what you might be asked after you bring your baby home and some suggestions on how you might respond (witty-wise style, of course).

Q: How much did your baby cost?
A: We paid for an adoption process, not a baby.

Q: Now that you've adopted, will you try to have your own children?
A: She is my own child.

Q: What country is your child from? (This happens a lot in transracial adoption when it's assumed a child of color must have been adopted internationally.)
A: Kansas. (Or whatever state or city your child is from.)

Q: Why did his parents give him up?
A: (Silence.)

Q: Was she born drug addicted?
A: No. Were you?

Q: How old is his mom?
A: I'm 34. (Insert your own age. If you want to be funny, "But clearly I don't look a day over twenty!")

Q: Are your children real siblings?
A: Well, they aren't imaginary siblings.[68]

Q: Aren't you afraid his birth parents will try to take him back?
A: Our adoption was legal and ethical.

Q: How could someone give away such a gorgeous baby?
A: (Walks away before offering free throat punch.)

Q: Are you going to tell her she's adopted?
A: Um, you just did.

Q: Do you think adopting is a good idea?
A: Is asking that question a good idea?

---

68 What an extraordinary answer, inspired by the children's book *A Family Is a Family Is a Family* by Sara O'Leary (2016). I highly recommend this title!

(Note: these questions may also come in the form of statements. Instead of, "Why did his parents give him up?" you might get, "I could never give my baby away to strangers." And of course, the statements such as, "Your child is so lucky you adopted her" and "God bless you for giving a child-in-need a good home." These come across as compliments and are usually not malicious, but they are nevertheless often inaccurate.)

Please note, a great go-to response to any question or comment can be: "It sounds like you're interested in adoption. Here is my adoption agency's information if you'd like to learn more." (And by all means, carry cards in your wallet!)

Now, how you respond is really up to you. Often it's situational, including where you are and who is asking, but it's also about your personality. Are you sarcastic? Direct? Humorous? As your child gets older, he or she should certainly weigh-in on these situations. How would the child like you to respond? Would he or she prefer to handle it?

Other options include changing the subject or simply walking away, which yes, I've actually done. A few years ago, my family and I were exiting our row of seats after my daughter's basketball game when a woman blocked us and began firing intrusive adoption questions while both of my oldest children stood on either side of me. Her physical stance (and proximity to us), as well as her question phrasing were inappropriate at best. I looked her right in the eyes and said, "That is none of your business." And then we walked away.

Now I know what you're thinking: I could never be that bold. Is it not rude to walk away from someone, change the subject, or refuse to answer their inquiries? My answer is: They started it. Seriously. Taking it back to first grade arguments. Honey, they started it. They approached you and decided that they deserved to know personal information about your child. Your child!

Still not convinced that you can shut down the busybody? Here's an analogy for ya.

You don't want up to someone in a wheelchair and say: *Wow! You're in a wheelchair! How much did your wheelchair cost? I bet it was super expensive. How did you afford it? Were you in an accident, or were you born this way? What, exactly, is wrong with you? Can you walk? Mind if*

I touch your wheelchair? Have you considered some sort of herbal treatment to heal your legs?

Of course you wouldn't do that.

I know, some of us (myself included) are passionate about adoption, and we sure love our babies. I mean, is there a better baby in the world than yours? No! But this doesn't mean you channel that passion and love into dishing out personal info like a cafeteria lady dishes out the mashed potatoes and gravy.

Now when I was new to motherhood, I mistakenly would give in and tell strangers too much. It was out of excitement and joy, but it wasn't right. I was trying to please others, to prove myself as a new mom (one who had obviously adopted her child) instead of holding the sacred sacred. Luckily, with time and education, I generated better responses.

Once you become a mom, your number one obligation is to your child. You have the honor of being part, *a part*, of an incredible and intricate story, one that you are not at the center of. Now this doesn't mean you are stuck up or secretive, it just means you are doing the job you were chosen to do: protect that baby.

Today my goal is to teach my children that their story belongs to them. Even though I am their mom and an adult (who has a whole lot of say-so), I respect their right to decide how and when and to whom the story is told. Furthermore, by shutting-down strangers' nosy questions and comments, I am demonstrating to my children that adults do not have the right to use their status, size, or age to bully answers out of our family. (And in the case of transracial adoption, there are the hair-touchers, which also presents a stranger-awareness issue. This is a great opportunity to teach children that their bodies belong to them. Microaggressions be damned.) Not only are you protecting the privacy of your child and your family, but the birth family as well.

Ladies, society conditions us to be polite and passive in order to please others. You are not a snob or a B because you stand up for your babies.

Anytime a situation arises where a stranger encroaches on your family's personal space, I want you to remember that junior high cheer: BE AGGRESSIVE, B-E AGGRESSIVE. Now change that up to what all us mamas need to be for our children: BE ASSERTIVE, B-E ASSERTIVE.

The Five Magic Words

"Please" and "thank you" aren't the only magic words.

You will, at some point or another, encounter those who oppose your choice to adopt or your decisions within that choice, such as your openness to a child of color or an ongoing relationship with the child's birth family. You know who I'm talking about: the nay-sayers, the haters, the Debbie Downers.

These aren't your "concerned" nearest-and-dearest. Certainly, open and honest conversations with those you are close to is important. You don't abandon ship because of a single drop of rain. But there are those (who could very well be in your inner circle, but also strangers who think they're worthy of offering commentary) who are going to ignorantly protest to your adoption choices. These might be strangers, friends and family, co-workers, and my personal favorite, strangers on the Internet.

Last year, I wrote an article for *Babble*, Disney's parenting website, called "The One Thing I Say to Shut Down the Mom-Shamers." What the article could have been titled, and the secret I'm going to share with you in this short-and-sweet chapter is, "The Five Magic Words for Anyone Dancin' On Your Last Nerve."

Ready?

The five magic words are: "I'm OK with my choices."

Think about it. The five magic words convey, "I take responsibility for myself. And guess what? I'm cool. I'm happy. I'm confident. And your feelings and thoughts and opinions are irrelevant. Mic drop. Buh-bye." The simple, direct sentence also keeps you from saying something inappropriate, angry, or out-of-control. It's easy to memorize five words versus drumming up a response, be it snarky or graceful, each time an inappropriate question or comment is hurled at you.

Try it! For anything: adoption related, parenting related, or your sister-in-law's condescending comment about your decision to vaccinate your future child.

Shut 'em down, girl. Shut. 'em. Down.

Go Big or Go Home

Let's have a girlfriend chat about open adoption.

So about ten years ago, open adoption was emerging. And like many hopeful parents, I was fearful. We swiftly checked "semi-open" on our adoption paperwork and moved on. We felt it was best. A way to straddle the fence. Nothing too intense. We'd move forward with our new baby, and the baby's birth mother would move on with her life. We'd send each other pictures and letters, via the adoption agency, and life would be good. No, life would be great.

We made our decision out of ignorance. We based our choice on stereotypes, pride, and fear. We were trying to protect our own hearts and make very very sure that we were Mom and Dad.

Now if you've read my blog or articles, you know we have four open adoptions. So what changed, you might ask?

Meeting birth parents. And it started not with our children's birth families, but with others. The summer before we adopted, my husband and I took a wonderfully long beach vaca. While at the airport waiting for our next flight, we heard a very young baby crying (that very, very distinct newborn cry). The noise got louder and louder, until a young lady plopped down in a seat near us, a hysterically hungry baby in her arms. She was soon joined by an older man. The baby was eating contently, when I leaned over and said to her, "You have a beautiful son."

She proceeded to tell us that she was going to place him for adoption. She's a young, single mom, trying to make it as a part-time hair stylist. The baby's father isn't involved. She put the baby in interim care for a week when she decided she couldn't place him. Her father, the man who was with her, promised to help support her, and she brought her baby boy home.

That woman was a face to a label, a possibility: birth mother. A birth mother is a real woman, ya'll. A person with feelings and struggles and victories and a family.

During that same vacation, my husband and I decided one evening to go putt-putt golfing. We got stuck on the course behind a very large and multiracial family. We caught tidbits of their conversations as we worked our way through the course. After, I went up to one of the adults in the group, unable to contain myself, and blurted, "We're waiting to adopt."[69]

The man looked at us kindly and smiled. Then the oldest child, who was probably about ten, lined up the children Von Trapp family style, and introduced us to each child. "This is Joel," and he pointed to a brown skinned, thick haired little boy and continued quite matter-of-fact, "We got him in Guatemala." He moved down the line, through all eight children. Turns out the children were comprised of two families, coming together for a cousin vacation. Then the oldest boy said, "Oh, and we have another one in the car napping with mom."

Their openness, their transparency, their candidness, their confidence, it was eye-opening and encouraging. They were who they were. And we knew, we knew, we would choose some degree of open adoption beyond just pictures and letters.

Fast-forward to today, and the pendulum has swung the other way. Open adoption is the norm. In fact, many agencies and adoption professionals expect families, sometimes even requiring them, to choose open adoption.

Here are my observations and experiences regarding open adoption. These are not hard-and-fast rules or adoption gospel. (Remember, I told you that no one person is the authority on adoption!) My hope is that these help you as you make decisions and navigate your journey:

---

69 Not polite. But I was new to adoption and really, really excited.

1: Open adoption isn't co-parenting.

When the legalities are done (TPR, revocation period over, finalization), the baby is your baby. Now this doesn't mean that you can't ask the child's birth parents for input. But the parenting duties and responsibilities are yours.

If you sense that an adoption professional is presenting open adoption as co-parenting or as a perfect solution, beware. Some agencies have used this tactic to lure expectant mothers into placing their babies, attempting to minimize the loss involved.

2: Open adoption eliminates some secrecy and shame.

When the situation surrounding the placement (history) and ongoing communication is in place, by default, some of the secrecy and shame surrounding the adoption fall away. There isn't a need for a big reveal, a lengthy search, or extensive wondering, because the answers are already laid out (or the questions can be asked).

Notice I said that openness eliminates "some" of the secrecy and shame. Triad members can still have struggles even though the adoption is open. Again, open adoption isn't a perfect solution or easy-as-pie[70] relationship.

3: Open adoption requires commitment.

Just like any relationship, challenges arise. Miscommunication happens. Feelings get hurt. When there are multiple people trying to navigate a unique and fragile relationship, there will be peaks and valleys. This is when everyone needs to remember the promises made to one another and stick to them, committing to working through any hardships that arise.

Speaking of commitment, I urge families not to make long-term promises. Yes, you read that correctly. I think it's short-sided to insist that you will force your child to visit his or her birth mother three times a year from birth until age eighteen, for example. There are so many factors that could mean a change in plans, including someone moving away, a deal-breaker, or the child not wanting to have visits.

---

70 Here I go with the carb references again!

Make short-term, healthy, realistic promises to one another. And when you make a promise, keep it. No excuses.

4: Open adoption requires flexibility.

People change. Relationships change. If you plan to treat the open adoption with sterile hands and a cold heart, it's not going to work. There are no rules surrounding open adoption, no guidebook. Each adoption, each person is different.

Furthermore, say you are committed to an open adoption, but the birth mother doesn't want it. That can be difficult and hurtful, yet you'll need to remain flexible. Your job is to keep the door open and always, always be honest and empathetic with your child.

5: Open adoption is three-sided.

The adoption triad (remember that's the adoptee, the parents, and the birth parents) all need to be participants when the child is still a child. Everyone needs to pull their weight in order for the relationship to be successful. This doesn't mean you have permission to bail at the first sign of struggle; however, it does mean that sometimes there's going to be some come-to-Jesus conversations about expectations, perceptions, commitments, and emotions.

6: Open adoptions take time.

Let the relationship grow organically. You know what happens when you harvest crops too early? They aren't great quality. They don't meet expectations. Too many families are so excited to be matched or placed, that they throw caution to the wind, become besties with the birth family, and then realize that wasn't such a great idea. Don't meet someone and go get matching hibiscus flower tats a week later. Be smart, be honest, and be open to growth and change.

7: Openness doesn't mean the placement will happen.

Refer back to point #6. During a match, a family and an expectant parent might grow very close. I'm not saying that is right or wrong. There might be sonograms and baby showers and even weekends spent together. The expectant mom might ask the family to be present at the birth, to cut the umbilical cord, to feed the baby at the hospital, to name the baby. These are intimate, sacred moments. But these are not promises that the baby will become yours. No matter how insistent a mom is, if and until she opts to place, the baby is hers.

8: <u>Openness requires transparency starting with the match.</u>

Do not make promises you don't intend to keep or are uncertain about. Naturally, adoption and openness can be uncomfortable. But if an expectant mother insinuates she'd like to be at all the child's birthday parties, and you aren't comfortable with this, you need to say so. Yes, that means the mother may choose a different family. But it is crucial that you are your authentic self and present yourself in an honest light. Not every possible match is a good fit for you.

Above all, the child should be at the center of the open adoption. As he or she gets older, the child should have a lot of say-so in what happens in the relationship. The adults need to remember that it isn't all about them. It's called the adoption triad for a reason: because each side of the triangle matters.

As you are trying to decide what feels right to you in terms of openness, I implore you to make decisions out of education and not ignorance. Lori Holden wrote an excellent book called *The Open Hearted Way to Open Adoption*. What I love about Lori's book is that her daughter's birth mother contributes her thoughts and experiences. This is one resource I encourage families to explore as they are choosing the level of openness in their future child's adoption.

Wow. That's eight points. And some sub-points. I'm tired of typing. You're tired of reading. Mandatory latte break, friend.

That's a Wrap

Wrapping up an adoption journey feels really, really good. Finalization is a legal declaration that the child is officially yours, forever.

Finalization rules vary state to state and by circumstance. Some finalize in a matter of weeks after placement, while some wait months, sometimes a year or longer. Finalizations might occur in person or over the phone (or video chat). Some families opt to include many friends and family, while others simply have the immediate family present. There really is no right or wrong way to finalize, just check with your attorney or social worker first and find out what the court's guidelines are.

After finalization you will receive your child's amended birth certificate (stating your name as the parent and the name you gave the child). Once you receive this, you can claim the adoption tax credit (the following tax filing season), get your child a social security number, and claim any additional adoption reimbursement you qualify for, such as through your employer.

Adoption is always complicated and bittersweet, but I want you to know that it's OK to be happy your child is forever yours. It's OK to rejoice in your fabulous family. And it's OK to celebrate.

Gotcha

Let's start with this: Yes, our family celebrates our kids' Gotcha Days. Before you start tweeting me, hold on. Hear me out.

Three and four and five (plus) years ago, we didn't celebrate our kids' Gotcha Days. I was adamantly opposed. I mean, it was, according to the Internet, essentially celebrating the severing of a birth family, and anyone celebrating such a day was certainly a clueless imbecile who coated adoption loss in cotton candy and glittery butterflies.

Then two years ago, I was having a heart-to-heart with a friend who is both an adoptee and a mom-by-adoption. I told her, of course we do not celebrate Gotcha Day! And she said something that blew. my. mind. She replied: "Um, why not?"

She shared how her mom made a big deal out of her day. Presents. A special outfit. A nice meal and dessert. A day of just celebrating her beautiful, smart, talented, kind self. It was as close to a birthday celebration as it could get. And guess what? SHE LOVED IT.

And I thought, have I been denying my kids something really cool? To alleviate some sort of guilt? To attempt to be super respectful of birth families with whom we love dearly, even though they had never voiced that celebrating the children and their adoptions was wrong?

Silly. Silly Mommy. I really didn't have a good reason other than someone I don't know and will never meet told me on the Internet that Gotcha Day is one of the ultimate adoption sins, and committing means I'm a heartless beast.

So I asked my children, *would you like to do something special to celebrate your adoption? It would be the anniversary of when we finalized your adoption, when you became a Garlinghouse forever. What do you think?*

The answer was an overwhelming, resounding yes.

And so I swallowed my doubt and said, OK. I marked their adoption finalization dates on the calendar. On their days, we gave them a small gift and made a special dessert.

And they, like my friend, LOVED it. They spent their entire days grinning ear-to-ear, reminding everyone around them it was their SPECIAL DAY.

So here's where I'm at: I'm totally open to the celebration changing, going away, or becoming bigger and better. I'm open to whatever each of my children needs and desires, individually.

You know why? Because as my friend Madeleine tells us in her book *Dear Adoptive Parents, What You Need to Know Right Now From an Adoptee*, we need to do our job. She gives us "permission slips" to BE the mother and father our children need. That's what being a good parent is: meeting the child's needs. (Please, please, please, read the book. I cannot tell you how much I learned from her words, how encouraged I felt, and how refreshing it was!)

So I'm going to keep doing that. I'm going to consider, of course, the experiences of others. Absolutely. Had I of not done that, we wouldn't have considered celebrating adoption finalizations in the first place. And I'm going to do the job I was chosen to do: raise my children, encourage them, support them, listen to them, empathize with them, and love them for exactly who they are. And of course, we're going to celebrate their fabulous selves without worrying anymore about what is "correct" and instead, what is right for each child.

Oh, and we do not, in fact, call it "Gotcha Day" for a few reasons. First, I hate "gotcha." It's creepy. It's like sneaking up behind someone and grabbing them while yelling "BOO!" No. We call adoption days, "Adoption Day," because it's simple, it's direct, and it is what it is. The end. I know some others prefer to call it Family Day.

Take it from Madeleine: Whatever your child wants and needs is what is right.

Happily Ever After

ey, friend.

You've made it. The last chapter. This is where I kick you (lovingly) out of the nest and watch you fly.

I'm proud of you. You've made a commitment to learn more about adoption so you can be an incredible mommy to the little one who will come your way.

I'm thankful for you. You have gone from a meandering, scared, hopeful parent who was eating wayyy too much ice cream to a stronger, more educated, more confident woman who is ready to embrace the motherhood to come. And you've done so by reading my book, sharing in my corner of the world. And you've left me comments and questions on social media, inviting me into your corner of the world. Thank you.

I'm excited for you. I'm cheering for you. Like right now. As I type this final chapter, my baby girl is on my lap, slobbering on my arm, grabbing at my keyboard, and taking breaks to gift me a toothy-grin. I am head-over-heels for this kid. And I can't wait for you to experience this same feeling.

I'm waiting for you. Send me an e-mail or a message on social media. Tell me where your head and heart are. Share happy news. Ask questions. Send me a link to the latest adoption-minded graphic tee (I'm obsessed with graphic tees) or completely off-topic Ryan Gosling meme ("Hey, girl."). Tell me a funny story. Send me a pic of your beautiful baby. We need one another so desperately, because this journey is way too lonely and crazy to travel alone.

Finally, I believe in you. I know that after reading all these chapters, you are committed to an ethical adoption. You may have doubts and fears and questions, but you aren't going to waiver. You are strong and smart. You are eagerly anticipating the news that you are a mommy-by-adoption. You are ready. Willing. Your arms, your mind, and your heart? They are wide-open.

Please keep being your authentic, courageous, enlightened self. Be present, curious, and sincere in your journey to motherhood. And above all, love your sweet baby with reckless abandon while you parent with both wit and wisdom.

Made in the USA
Middletown, DE
18 July 2021

44368996R00116